—Real food
recipes for your
Frying Pan

— Real Food —
recipes for your
Frying Pan

Carolyn Humphries

foulsham

LONDON • NEW YORK • TORONTO • SYDNEY

foulsham

The Publishing House, Bennetts Close, Cippenham,
Slough, Berkshire, SL1 5AP, England

ISBN 0-572-02813-X

Copyright © 2002 W. Foulsham & Co. Ltd

Cover photograph © by Peter Howard Smith

Printed in Great Britain by Cox & Wyman Ltd, Reading, Berkshire

Contents

Introduction

Using a frying pan (skillet) is my favourite way to cook. It's quick, versatile and nutritious. Think of the Chinese wok: it cooks fast, using the minimum of oil, and produces colourful, tasty results. Your frying pan can do the same. Say goodbye to lard (shortening) and dripping, say hello to seed, nut and vegetable oils – and even to no fat at all!

But stir-fries are just the beginning. With a frying pan, you can cook everything from sensational starters and snacks to complete meat, fish, poultry and vegetarian main meals, as well as side dishes and the most delicious assortment of desserts, breads and teatime treats. Then there are breakfasts too – and I don't mean fry-ups swimming in fat, but taste-tingling, original creations to set you up for the day.

I can't pretend that every single recipe is a dieter's delight. But there are some things that are just too good to miss – even if they are wicked. Take my Pan-oh-chocolat, for instance. A crisp, golden crescent, oozing liquid chocolate, richer and puffier than its French counterpart, it's simple to make and so divine – and everyone's allowed a treat from time to time!

Most of the recipes are for four people, but they can be quartered or halved easily if you are cooking for one or two. So, whether you live in a bedsit or studio flat with just two rings to cook on or you have a family to feed, your trusty frying pan can be your best asset in the kitchen, bringing you speedy results with lots of flavour and a huge reduction on your fuel bills.

Cooking in Your Frying Pan

Cooking in a frying pan (skillet) couldn't be simpler. The golden rule is always to heat the pan before adding the food. If you are using oil or any other fat, you must heat that too or it will simply soak into the food as it cooks, giving soggy, greasy results. The food will also stick to the base and the results will be disappointing, at the very least, and quite possibly inedible!

When cooking in butter, I often add a little oil as well. This is to stop the butter turning black and burning, and will give you the lovely flavour of butter with the crisp, golden results of oil. You can use margarine, if you prefer, but as it has a higher water content you may find it spits a lot, and food is more likely to stick to the pan unless you use oil too.

Dry-frying is an excellent method of cooking foods that already have a high fat content, such as bacon, sausages and minced (ground) meat. As the food cooks, the fat runs out and helps it to cook without sticking. But you must turn or stir regularly, or it will burn. I also use a dry pan for some breads, giving a crisp outside with a soft, spongy interior. The dough should be well floured or dusted with another grain to act as a barrier between the hot pan and the bread and, again, to help prevent burning.

Choosing frying pans

Ideally, you should have several pans: a small omelette pan for omelettes, pancakes and small quantities to serve one or two people; a medium-sized pan for standard cooking; and a larger, heavy-based one for larger fish and pieces of meat, and for stir-fries and deep-frying. Have at least one with a non-stick coating if you can, but it's not strictly necessary if your pans are good-quality, heavy-based ones, providing you season them well (see page 8).

Do buy the best-quality pans you can afford. Cheap ones will burn the food, smoke too quickly and stick and will always give disappointing results. More expensive, heavy pans will last you for years.

Griddles

As an alternative to frying pans, griddles are great! A griddle is a ridge-based cast-iron pan for searing steaks, chops etc., that gives a characteristic charred, lined appearance to the food. Treat yourself – it'll give you professional, appetising results.
Top tip: When using a griddle, don't oil the griddle, oil the food. Heat the dry griddle until very hot. Brush the steak, etc. with oil and add to the pan. Cook for exactly half the time on each side, so you turn it only once. You'll get perfect lines on the food and will have used no excess fat.

Seasoning your pan

Before you use any pan for the first time, season it. Heat 30–45 ml/2–3 tbsp oil in it until it smokes. Leave it to cool, then wipe it out with kitchen paper (paper towels). This will prevent food sticking and will ensure great results every time.

Cleaning your pans

When you have finished deep- or shallow-frying in oil, you may find that you need only to pour off the used oil and then wipe out the pan with kitchen paper (paper towels). But when it needs serious cleaning, use hot detergent water and a non-metallic scourer. **Never** use wire wool or you will scratch the base and your food will stick. Use nothing coarser than a plastic washing-up brush on Teflon-coated non-stick pans. When you have washed your pan thoroughly, wipe it round with a tiny drop of oil on a piece of kitchen paper to re-season the surface.

Two-ring tips

If you have only two rings to cook on, with no oven to keep things warm, don't despair. If my recipe suggests keeping part of a dish warm in a low oven while cooking something else, simply put the food on a plate over a pan of gently simmering water and cover with a lid instead.

Also, if you want to brown the tops of dishes but you don't have a grill (broiler), buy yourself a cook's blowtorch. A quick blast over the surface is all it takes – and it's great fun to use!

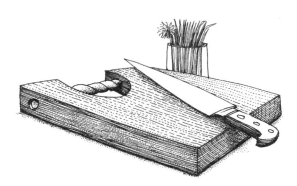

A Well-stocked Storecupboard

*I*f you keep a good stock of basic food items in your kitchen cupboard, you will be ready to cook up a feast at the drop of a hat without having to rush out to buy everything first. The list below is meant as a general guide. Adapt it to suit your own requirements and individual tastes, of course!

Packets, bottles and jars

◇ Baking powder
◇ Bicarbonate of soda (baking soda)
◇ Clear honey
◇ Cocoa (unsweetened chocolate) powder
◇ Dried fruit – raisins, sultanas (golden raisins), currants, dried mixed fruit (fruit cake mix), ready-to-eat apricots, prunes and/or other soft fruits
◇ Dried herbs – basil, chives, oregano, thyme, mint, sage and mixed herbs
◇ Dried (non-fat dry) milk
◇ Dried minced (ground) onion and dried red and green (bell) peppers – not vital but great for brightening up rice or pasta and they keep for ages
◇ Drinking (sweetened) chocolate powder – I use an instant chocolate drink powder containing milk powder
◇ Flour – plain (all-purpose), self-raising (self-rising) and wholemeal
◇ Garlic – a tube of purée (paste) makes a good alternative to fresh garlic; use about 1 cm/½ in per garlic clove
◇ Horseradish – relish, sauce or cream
◇ Instant coffee powder or granules
◇ Lemon juice
◇ Marmalade
◇ Marmite or other yeast extract
◇ Mayonnaise
◇ Mustard – made English, Dijon and grainy

◇ Oil – sunflower and olive for general cooking and dressings; groundnut (peanut) or corn for deep-frying; speciality oils, such as sesame and walnut, to be used sparingly for extra flavour

◇ Passata (sieved tomatoes)

◇ Pasta – spaghetti, lasagne sheets, stuffed tortellini, quick-cook macaroni and/or other shapes

◇ Pepper – black peppercorns, for grinding in a mill, and ready-ground white

◇ Preserves – redcurrant jelly (clear conserve) and mint and cranberry sauces

◇ Rice – long-grain (preferably basmati) and risotto rice (I use arborio)

◇ Salt

◇ Spices – ground cayenne and/or chilli powder, cinnamon, ginger, cumin, coriander (cilantro), etc.; whole or ready-grated nutmeg

◇ Stock cubes – vegetable, chicken and beef

◇ Sugar – caster (superfine), granulated, light and dark brown

◇ Table sauces – brown, Worcestershire, Tabasco, soy and chilli, and tomato ketchup (catsup)

◇ Tomato purée (paste) – tubes keep better than jars

◇ Vinegar – red or white wine or cider, balsamic, malt

Cans

◇ Baked beans

◇ Corned beef and/or ham

◇ Custard

◇ Fish – anchovies, mackerel, pilchards or sardines, salmon and tuna

◇ Fruits – any favourites; pineapple is particularly useful

◇ Pulses – red kidney beans, butter (lima) beans, cannellini beans, lentils, etc.

◇ Rice pudding

◇ Soups – condensed mushroom, chicken and tomato

◇ Vegetables – sweetcorn (corn), peas, carrots, green beans, mushrooms and tomatoes (chopped tomatoes are great for quick sauces)

Fridge

◇ Butter and/or margarine – I prefer a reduced-fat olive oil spread, suitable for cooking as well as spreading, for most uses, but I also keep butter for its flavour and hard block margarine and white vegetable fat for pastry (paste)

◇ Cheese – Cheddar and grated Parmesan, plus others as required

◇ Cream – single (light) and double (heavy) or whipping; long-life varieties are ideal for cooking

◇ Crème fraîche – the half-fat variety can be heated without curdling

◇ Eggs – medium for general cooking, large for boiling

◇ Plain yoghurt – good for sauces and dressings or to accompany cereals, fruits and desserts

Freezer

◇ Bread/rolls/pitta breads/naan, etc.

◇ Herbs – fresh chopped parsley, chives and coriander (cilantro) are particularly suitable for freezing

◇ Milk – keeps well in the freezer but remember it takes ages to thaw and will need a good shake once defrosted

◇ Prawns – free-flow frozen prawns are best as you can use as few or as many as you need

◇ Vegetables – peas and beans

Fresh fruit and vegetables

◇ Apples, bananas, oranges and lemons

◇ Potatoes, onions, carrots, mushrooms and salad stuffs

Notes on the Recipes

◇ Quantities are given in metric, imperial and American measures. Follow one set only.

◇ American terms are given in brackets.

◇ All spoon measures are level. 1 tsp = 5 ml; 1 tbsp = 15 ml.

◇ Eggs are medium unless otherwise stated. If you use a different size, adjust the amount of liquid added to obtain the right consistency.

◇ Always wash, peel, core and seed, if necessary, fresh foods before use. Ensure that all produce is as fresh as possible and in good condition.

◇ Seasoning and the use of strongly flavoured ingredients, such as spices and garlic, are very much a matter of personal taste. Taste the food as you cook and adjust the quantities to suit your own palate.

◇ Always use fresh herbs unless dried are specifically called for. If it is necessary to substitute dried, use half the quantity – or less. Chopped frozen varieties are much better than dried, but are not suitable as a garnish. Don't attempt to use dried parsley or coriander (cilantro) instead of fresh.

◇ A fresh bouquet garni is traditionally made up of sprigs of thyme, parsley and a bay leaf, tied together or wrapped in muslin (cheesecloth). Bouquet garni sachets of dried herbs are now readily available in supermarkets and are a good substitute.

◇ Can and packet sizes are approximate and will vary slightly according to the particular brand.

◇ All preparation and cooking times are approximate and intended as a guide only.

◇ I have specified sunflower or olive oil for most cooking in the recipes, but have suggested you use groundnut (peanut) or corn oil for deep-frying as they have a higher smoking temperature. You can use a seed oil or ordinary vegetable oil if you prefer. Don't use the same oil more than three times for deep-frying or the results will be disappointing.

◇ You can use either butter or margarine in the recipes. If using a reduced-fat margarine, check your brand is suitable for cooking as well as spreading.

◇ I've included various salad combinations as serving suggestions. Simply prepare the ingredients in your usual way and toss in a French dressing.

◇ Use your own discretion on substituting ingredients and personalising recipes. Make notes on particular successes as you go along.

◇ I have often called for a food processor or blender to speed up preparation, but use other kitchen gadgets as you like to make life easier.

◇ Most of the recipes are designed for four people but the quantities can be reduced easily to serve one or two.

Light Meals, Snacks and Breakfasts

*T*his chapter contains all sorts of delectable eats that are simple to prepare and quick to cook. Most are extremely good for you too, being low in fat, and quite a number make fantastic breakfasts – the perfect start to the day.

Remember, just because you use your frying pan (skillet) doesn't mean the food has to be swilling in fat and laden with unwanted calories. There are exceptions, of course, like the gorgeous, gooey filled croissants, but everyone deserves a little pampering sometimes!

Pan-scrambled Eggs with Smoked Salmon
SERVES 4

The pan-scrambled eggs are also delicious plain. If you are reducing this recipe to cook for one, use one large or two small eggs, according to your appetite.

25 g/1 oz/2 tbsp butter or margarine
6 eggs
Salt and freshly ground black pepper
30 ml/2 tbsp milk or single (light) cream
100 g/4 oz smoked salmon pieces
A squeeze of lemon juice
4 slices of wholemeal bread, toasted and buttered
15 ml/1 tbsp snipped fresh chives

① Melt the butter or margarine in a frying pan (skillet) until foaming. Meanwhile, break the eggs into a bowl and whisk in just a pinch of salt, lots of pepper and the milk or cream.

② Pour the egg mixture into the pan and cook over a moderate heat, stirring all the time until half scrambled.

③ Scatter in the smoked salmon pieces and add a squeeze of lemon juice. Stir until scrambled but still slightly creamy.

④ Meanwhile, make the toast. Pile the egg and salmon mixture on to the hot buttered toast and sprinkle with the chives before serving.

PREPARATION TIME: 3 MINUTES
COOKING TIME: 5 MINUTES

Speciality Hash Browns
SERVES 4

*It's worth cooking more potatoes than you need for a main
meal just so you can make this delicious dish.
For minimum fuss, prepare the cakes in advance (steps 1–2),
then, when required, just dip in batter and cook.
They're also a great accompaniment to any fried (sautéed)
or grilled (broiled) fish, meat or poultry.*

Sunflower oil, for cooking
1 large onion, chopped
450 g/1 lb leftover cooked potatoes, chopped
15 ml/1 tbsp poppy seeds
Salt and freshly ground black pepper
50 g/2 oz/½ cup self-raising (self-rising) flour
120 ml/4 fl oz/½ cup water
To serve:
Tomato ketchup (catsup) or brown table sauce

① Heat 15 ml/1 tbsp oil in a frying pan (skillet) and fry the
onion for 3 minutes until softened. Tip into a bowl and
mash in the potatoes and poppy seeds. Season well with
salt and pepper.

② Shape the mixture into square cakes.

③ Wipe out the frying pan with kitchen paper (paper towels).

④ Mix the flour with the water and a pinch of salt to a smooth
thick batter.

⑤ Heat enough oil to coat the base of a large frying pan. Dip
the cakes in the batter, then fry in the hot oil for 2–3 minutes
on each side until crisp and golden. Drain on kitchen paper
and serve with tomato ketchup or brown sauce.

PREPARATION TIME: 6 MINUTES
COOKING TIME: 4–6 MINUTES

Cod's Roe with Lemon and Anchovy Butter

SERVES 4

2 x 200 g/7 oz/small cans of pressed cod's roe
50 g/2 oz/½ cup plain (all-purpose) flour
1.5 ml/¼ tsp cayenne
Salt and freshly ground black pepper
4 soft rolls
50 g/2 oz/¼ cup butter
Finely grated rind of 1 lemon
5 ml/1 tsp anchovy essence (extract)
Sunflower oil, for cooking
A few sprigs of fresh parsley

① Slice each can of roe into six slices.

② Mix the flour, cayenne and a little salt and pepper on a plate. Dip the cod's roe in the flour mixture to coat completely.

③ Preheat the oven to low. Wrap the bread rolls in foil and put in the oven to warm. Mix the butter, lemon rind, anchovy essence and a good grinding of black pepper in an ovenproof bowl. Place in the oven to melt.

④ Heat just enough oil to cover the base of a large frying pan (skillet), then fry (sauté) half the slices for about 3 minutes on each side until golden brown. Drain on kitchen paper (paper towels). Keep warm in the oven while cooking the remainder.

⑤ Transfer the roe slices to warm plates. Trickle the melted butter mixture around and garnish with sprigs of parsley. Serve with the warm rolls.

PREPARATION TIME: 5 MINUTES
COOKING TIME: 12 MINUTES (6 MINUTES PER BATCH)

Devilled Kidneys
SERVES 4

This was a favourite breakfast dish for the Victorians.
It also makes a delicious lunch or supper.

8 lambs' kidneys
15 g/½ oz/1 tbsp butter or margarine
4 rashers (slices) of streaky bacon, rinded and diced
1.5 ml/¼ tsp chilli powder
45 ml/3 tbsp tomato ketchup (catsup)
30 ml/2 tbsp Worcestershire sauce
10 ml/2 tsp malt vinegar
5 ml/1 tsp made English mustard
10 ml/2 tsp demerara sugar
Salt and freshly ground black pepper
4 slices of white bread, toasted and cut into triangles
A few sprigs of fresh parsley

① Cut the kidneys into halves and snip out the central cores with scissors. Cut each half into two or three pieces.

② Heat the butter or margarine in a frying pan (skillet) until foaming. Add the kidneys and bacon and fry (sauté) for 3–4 minutes until cooked but the kidneys are still just pink.

③ Add all the remaining ingredients except the toasted bread and parsley sprigs, and season to taste with salt and pepper. Allow to bubble for 2 minutes, stirring all the time.

④ Spoon on to warm plates. Arrange the toast triangles around and garnish with sprigs of parsley.

PREPARATION TIME: 5 MINUTES
COOKING TIME: 5–6 MINUTES

American Pancakes with Maple Syrup

MAKES 8 PANCAKES

Serve these with bacon as well, as the Americans do,
if you like.

100 g/4 oz/1 cup plain (all-purpose) flour
2.5 ml/½ tsp salt
30 ml/2 tbsp caster (superfine) sugar
10 ml/2 tsp baking powder
1 small egg
25 g/1 oz//2 tbsp butter, melted
200 ml/7 fl oz/scant 1 cup milk
Sunflower oil, for cooking
To serve:
Maple syrup

① Sift the flour, salt, caster sugar and baking powder together in a bowl.

② Beat the egg with the melted butter and milk and gradually work into the flour mixture to form a thick batter.

③ Heat a little oil in a frying pan (skillet) and pour off the excess. Add enough batter to make a 12.5 cm/5 in pancake. Cook until golden underneath and bubbles are breaking on the surface. Flip over and cook the other side. Keep warm in a napkin while making the remainder.

④ Serve the pancakes hot with maple syrup trickled over.

PREPARATION TIME: 5 MINUTES
COOKING TIME: ABOUT 20 MINUTES (2–3 MINUTES PER PANCAKE)

Kipper Kedgeree
SERVES 4

This is traditionally made with yellow smoked fish but I think that the rich smokiness of kippers tastes even better.

2 eggs
2 kipper fillets, about 75 g/3 oz each
15 ml/1 tbsp sunflower oil
15 g/½ oz/1 tbsp butter or margarine
1 small onion, chopped
175 g/6 oz/¾ cup long-grain rice
600 ml/1 pt/2½ cups chicken or vegetable stock
50 g/2 oz frozen peas
A pinch of freshly grated nutmeg
Salt and freshly ground black pepper
30 ml/2 tbsp chopped fresh parsley

① Scrub the eggs in their shells under cold, running water, then wrap each in foil.

② Skin the kipper fillets and cut into bite-sized pieces.

③ Heat the oil and butter or margarine in a large frying pan (skillet). Add the onion and cook, stirring, for 2 minutes. Add the rice and stir until glistening.

④ Pour on the stock and bring to the boil, stirring. Add the foil-wrapped eggs, bring back to the boil, then cover the pan with foil or a lid, reduce the heat and cook for 5 minutes.

⑤ Add the fish, peas and nutmeg, stir, re-cover and cook for a further 5 minutes or until the rice is tender and has absorbed all the liquid.

⑥ Lift the eggs out of the pan. Remove the foil and rinse under cold water. Remove the shells and cut the eggs into quarters. Stir the rice mixture, season to taste and add the eggs and parsley. Serve straight from the pan.

PREPARATION TIME: 5 MINUTES
COOKING TIME: 15 MINUTES

Tortilla Special
SERVES 4

A tortilla, or traditional Spanish omelette, is made with thinly sliced potatoes and onion, but this recipe offers a colourful and tasty alternative. Pimenton is a smoky-flavoured sweet red pepper. Use paprika instead if you like, but you won't get such an exciting taste.

45 ml/3 tbsp olive oil
1 large potato, scrubbed and thinly sliced
1 large onion, thinly sliced
1 green (bell) pepper, thinly sliced
1 garlic clove, crushed
1.5 ml/¼ tsp pimenton
6 eggs
Salt and freshly ground black pepper
4 sliced tomatoes

① Heat the oil in a large frying pan (skillet). Add the potato, onion and pepper and stir over a gentle heat until coated in the oil. Cover with a lid, keep the heat low and cook for 6 minutes until tender, stirring once or twice.

② Add the garlic and pimenton and cook, stirring, for a further 30 seconds.

③ Beat the eggs with a little salt and pepper and pour into the pan. Turn up the heat to moderately high and cook, lifting and stirring gently, until the base is golden and the omelette is set.

④ Place the pan under a preheated grill (broiler) until the top is golden. Alternatively, invert the pan over a plate to tip the omelette out, then slide it back in the pan, browned-side up, to cook the other side for a minute or two.

⑤ Cut into wedges and serve garnished with the tomato slices.

PREPARATION TIME: 10 MINUTES
COOKING TIME: 10–12 MINUTES

Piperade with Garlic and Peppers
SERVES 4

Serve this with lots of crusty bread and a green salad for an excellent lunch or supper dish. If cooking for one, use one large or two small eggs and flavour with one whole (bell) pepper of any colour.

---

25 g/1 oz/2 tbsp butter or margarine
15 ml/1 tbsp olive oil
1 large onion, sliced
1 red pepper, thinly sliced
1 green pepper, thinly sliced
1 yellow pepper, thinly sliced
1 orange pepper, thinly sliced
1 large garlic clove, crushed
2 beefsteak tomatoes, roughly chopped
6 eggs, beaten
Salt and freshly ground black pepper
15 ml/1 tbsp chopped fresh coriander (cilantro)

---

① Heat the butter or margarine with the oil in a large frying pan (skillet). Add the onion and peppers and cook, stirring, for 3 minutes until softened.

② Add the garlic and tomatoes and continue to cook and stir over a moderate heat for a further 2–3 minutes until everything is just tender.

③ Pour in the eggs, sprinkle with salt and pepper and the coriander. Cook, gently stirring, until scrambled. Serve straight from the pan.

PREPARATION TIME: 10 MINUTES
COOKING TIME: 9–10 MINUTES

Pan Pizza

SERVES 2–4

Traditionally, pizzas are baked in a clay oven but this version makes a quick and easy snack meal with no time needed for the dough to rise. You can add extra toppings of your choice before you add the cheese: try a handful of chopped ham, some slices of mushroom, a few anchovies, or some sweetcorn (corn) or tuna.

---

100 g/4 oz/1 cup self-raising (self-rising) flour
5 ml/1 tsp baking powder
Salt and freshly ground black pepper
60 ml/4 tbsp olive oil
90 ml/6 tbsp cold water
45 ml/3 tbsp tomato purée (paste)
2.5 ml/½ tsp dried oregano
75 g/3 oz/¾ cup Cheddar cheese, grated
2 tomatoes, sliced
3 black olives (optional)

---

① Mix the flour and baking powder with 1.5 ml/¼ tsp salt in a bowl. Stir in 30 ml/2 tbsp of the oil and mix with enough cold water to form a soft but not sticky dough.

② Knead gently on a lightly floured surface and roll out to a round the size of the base of a medium frying pan (skillet).

③ Heat just enough of the remaining oil to coat the base of the frying pan. Add the round of dough and cook for 3 minutes until golden underneath. Turn over.

④ Spread the tomato purée on top, then sprinkle with the oregano and then the cheese. Top with the tomato slices and olives, if liked, and season with black pepper. Trickle the remaining oil over. Cover and cook gently for 5 minutes until the cheese has melted. If liked, flash under a hot grill (broiler) to brown.

⑤ Serve straight from the pan, cut into wedges.

PREPARATION TIME: 8 MINUTES
COOKING TIME: 8 MINUTES

Fried Red Beef Sandwich

SERVES 1

When making fried (sautéed) sandwiches, the butter must be spread on the outside. You can, obviously, use the same method to make all your usual favourites – cheese, cheese and ham, cheese and tomato, corned beef and pickle and so on – but this one is sensational!

2 slices of white bread
Butter or margarine, for spreading
2.5 ml/½ tsp horseradish relish
2 slices of cold roast beef
30 ml/2 tbsp pickled red cabbage
Freshly ground black pepper

① Spread the slices of bread on one side with butter or margarine.

② Spread horseradish lightly on the other side and put the roast beef on top of the horseradish on one slice.

③ Drain the pickled cabbage on kitchen paper (paper towels), then spread over the beef and season with black pepper.

④ Top with the other slice of bread, buttered-side up.

⑤ Heat a frying pan (skillet) over a moderate heat. Add the sandwich and fry, pressing down lightly with a fish slice, until golden brown underneath. Carefully turn over and fry, pressing again, until golden. Don't have the heat too high or the sandwich will burn before the filling is hot.

⑥ Cut in half and serve straight away.

PREPARATION TIME: 3 MINUTES
COOKING TIME: 3–4 MINUTES

Vegetable Samosas

MAKES 30

It's worth making a whole batch of these delicious little snacks. They will keep in the fridge for several days or can be frozen for up to 3 months. If you wish to reheat them, thaw, if frozen, then heat in a preheated oven at 200°C/400°F/gas mark 6 (fan oven 180°C) for about 5 minutes or until crisp and piping hot.

25 ml/1½ tbsp sunflower oil
1 small onion, finely chopped
5 ml/1 tsp ground cumin
2.5 ml/½ tsp chilli powder
5 ml/1 tsp ground turmeric
5 ml/1 tsp garam masala
175 g/6 oz mashed potato
150 g/5 oz/1 small can of garden peas
15 ml/1 tbsp chopped fresh coriander (cilantro)
225 g/8 oz/2 cups plain (all-purpose) flour
2.5 ml/½ tsp salt
150–175 ml/5–6 fl oz/⅔–¾ cup cold water
A little beaten egg
Groundnut (peanut) or corn oil, for deep-frying

① Heat 15 ml/1 tbsp of the sunflower oil and fry (sauté) the onion, stirring, for 2 minutes. Add the spices and fry, stirring, for a further 1 minute. Mix in the potato, the entire contents of the can of peas and the coriander. Tip into a bowl and set on one side. Rinse out the pan.

② Sift the flour and salt into a bowl. Add the remaining 10 ml/ 2 tsp sunflower oil and mix with enough of the water to form a firm dough. Knead gently on a lightly floured surface and cut into 15 equal pieces. Roll into balls, then roll out each piece to a 12.5 cm/5 in round.

③ Cut each round in half and brush the edges with egg.

④ Spoon the filling into the centre of each semi-circle. Fold in one corner to the centre of the rounded edge. Fold the other corner over the first one to form a triangle. Press the edges together to seal.

⑤ Pour about 2 cm/¾ in of oil into the frying pan (skillet) and heat until a cube of day-old bread browns in 30 seconds. Cook the samosas in batches for about 4 minutes until golden brown, turning once if necessary. Turn down the heat if browning too quickly.

⑥ Drain on kitchen paper (paper towels). Serve hot or cold.

PREPARATION TIME: 15 MINUTES
COOKING TIME: 20–30 MINUTES (4 MINUTES PER BATCH)

Quick Pineapple Rice with Chicken
SERVES 4

The quantities for this are not vital – use whatever you have.

15 ml/1 tbsp sunflower oil
225 g/8 oz/2 cups cooked long-grain rice
100 g/4 oz/1 cup cooked chicken, diced
225 g/8 oz/1 small can of pineapple pieces
50 g/2 oz cooked peas
50 g/2 oz cooked carrots, diced
5 cm/2 in piece of cucumber, diced
30 ml/2 tbsp mayonnaise
A few drops of soy sauce
Freshly ground black pepper

① Heat the oil in a large frying pan (skillet). Add all the ingredients except the mayonnaise, soy sauce and pepper.

② Toss over a gentle heat for 4–5 minutes until piping hot.

③ Stir in the mayonnaise, soy sauce and pepper to taste and cook for a further 1 minute. Serve in warmed bowls.

PREPARATION TIME: 5 MINUTES
COOKING TIME: 5–6 MINUTES

Hot BLT Baguette

SERVES 1

*If you can't find sandwich baguettes, use
half a small French stick.*

---

1 sandwich baguette
15 ml/1 tbsp sunflower oil
3 rashers (slices) of smoked back bacon, rinded
1 tomato, sliced
1 flat mushroom, peeled and sliced
Freshly ground black pepper
30 ml/2 tbsp mayonnaise
2–3 lettuce leaves, shredded

---

① Warm the baguette in a low oven while cooking the filling.

② Heat the oil in a large frying pan (skillet). Add the bacon
and fry (sauté) for 2 minutes, then turn over and push to
one side of the pan.

③ Add the sliced tomato and mushroom and fry for a further
2 minutes or until the mushrooms and tomatoes are
cooked, turning them over once if necessary. Add a good
grinding of pepper.

④ Split the baguette down one side and spread with
mayonnaise. Fill with the bacon, tomato and mushroom
slices and add the shredded lettuce. Serve straight away.

PREPARATION TIME: 3 MINUTES
COOKING TIME: 4 MINUTES

Pan Panino
SERVES 1

1 part-baked sandwich baguette
15 ml/1 tbsp ready-made pesto sauce
15 ml/1 tbsp crème fraîche
1 thin slice of Parma ham
A small handful of rocket leaves
1 plum tomato, sliced
6 slivers of Parmesan cheese
5 ml/1 tsp sliced black olives
30 ml/2 tbsp olive oil

① Split the baguette down one side. Place between two chopping boards and press down to flatten the bread. Gently open up.

② Mix the pesto with the crème fraîche and spread inside. Tuck in a slice of ham, then fill with the rocket, tomato, Parmesan and olives.

③ Heat half the oil in a frying pan (skillet) over a moderate heat. Add the panino and fry (sauté) for about 3 minutes until golden underneath, pressing down occasionally with a fish slice.

④ Add the remaining oil. Carefully turn the bread over, and cook for a further 3 minutes or until the other side is golden and the panino is hot through, pressing down from time to time. Take care the heat is not too fierce or the bread will burn before the filling is hot.

⑤ Drain on kitchen paper (paper towels), then serve straight away.

PREPARATION TIME: 3 MINUTES
COOKING TIME: 6 MINUTES

Hot Croissant Melt

SERVES 1

Don't be in too much of a hurry – if you turn the heat up,
the croissant will burn.

---

1 large croissant
1 thin slice of ham
1 slice of Cheddar cheese
10 ml/2 tsp tomato relish
10 ml/¼ oz/2 tsp butter or margarine

---

① Split the croissant along one side. Tuck in the ham, then the cheese, cutting it to fit in a single layer, and add the tomato relish.

② Spread the butter or margarine all over the outside.

③ Heat a heavy-based frying pan (skillet), then turn the heat down low. Fry (sauté) the croissant gently for about 3 minutes on each side, moving it around the pan to prevent it from burning, until crisp and hot through. Serve straight away.

PREPARATION TIME: 2 MINUTES
COOKING TIME: 6 MINUTES

Crispy Polenta with Cheese and Pickles

SERVES 4

You need to buy ready-cooked polenta (cornmeal) in a slab for this dish.

500 g/18 oz/1 large pack of cooked polenta
60 ml/4 tbsp cornflour (cornstarch)
Salt and freshly ground black pepper
45 ml/3 tbsp olive oil
45 ml/3 tbsp freshly grated Parmesan cheese
4 pickled baby beets, quartered
8 gherkins (cornichons)
12 pickled silverskin (pearl) onions

① Cut the slab of polenta into 12 slices.

② Season the cornflour with salt and pepper and dip the slices in this to cover both sides.

③ Heat the oil in a frying pan (skillet). Add the polenta and fry (sauté) for 2–3 minutes on each side until crisp and golden brown. Drain on kitchen paper (paper towels).

④ Place on plates, sprinkle with the Parmesan and arrange the pickles on one side.

PREPARATION TIME: 3 MINUTES
COOKING TIME: 4–6 MINUTES

Rarebit on Rye
SERVES 2

Use beer, wine or apple juice instead of cider, if you prefer. If you make this for one person, use a small frying pan (skillet). If for four, you will have to cook the bread in two batches.

4 slices of dark rye bread
Butter or margarine, for spreading
175 g/6 oz/1½ cups Cheddar cheese, grated
5 ml/1 tsp made English mustard
30 ml/2 tbsp medium-sweet cider
A few sprigs of fresh parsley

① Spread the bread on both sides with a little butter or margarine. Heat a frying pan and fry (sauté) the bread on both sides to brown. Keep warm while cooking the rarebit.

② Wipe out the pan with a piece of kitchen paper (paper towel). Add the cheese, mustard and cider and heat gently, stirring all the time, until melted and blended.

③ Put the fried bread on warm plates. Spoon the cheese mixture on top and garnish with parsley. Serve straight away.

PREPARATION TIME: 4 MINUTES
COOKING TIME: 4 MINUTES

Poached Eggs on Savoury Toast

SERVES 4

15 g/½ oz/1 tbsp butter or margarine
25 g/1 oz/2 tbsp medium-fat soft cheese
5 ml/1 tsp anchovy essence (extract)
5 ml/1 tsp Marmite or other yeast extract
15 ml/1 tbsp lemon juice
4 eggs
4 slices of wholemeal bread

① Mash the butter or margarine with the cheese, anchovy essence and Marmite.

② Pour about 2.5 cm/1 in boiling water into a frying pan (skillet). Add the lemon juice. Bring back to the boil, then reduce the heat to a gentle simmer.

③ Break the eggs one at a time into a cup and gently slide into the water. Cover with a lid and poach for 3–5 minutes until cooked to your liking.

④ Meanwhile, toast the bread on both sides. Spread with the butter mixture.

⑤ Place on warm plates. Remove the eggs with a draining spoon and slide one on top of each piece of toast. Serve immediately.

PREPARATION TIME: 3 MINUTES
COOKING TIME: 4–6 MINUTES

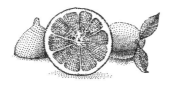

Cheesy Sausage Burgers
SERVES 4

These make a great snack at any time, but my family love them for breakfast, so I prepare and shape the patties (step 1) the night before, ready to cook in the morning.

225 g/8 oz pork sausagemeat
2 cup mushrooms, finely chopped
15 ml/1 tbsp chopped fresh parsley
30 ml/2 tbsp medium-fat soft cheese
Freshly ground black pepper
4 soft white rolls
5 ml/1 tsp sunflower oil

① Mash the sausagemeat in a bowl with the mushrooms, parsley and cheese. Season well with pepper. With lightly floured hands, shape the mixture into four flattish cakes, about the size of the rolls. Chill until ready to cook.

② Split the rolls, wrap in foil and warm in a low oven.

③ Brush the base of a large frying pan (skillet) with the oil and heat. Add the sausage burgers and fry (sauté) over a moderate heat for about 5 minutes on each side until golden brown and cooked through. Transfer to the warm rolls and serve straight away.

PREPARATION TIME: 8 MINUTES PLUS CHILLING
COOKING TIME: 10 MINUTES

The Perfect Omelette
SERVES 1

Without doubt, the simplest snack meal there is.

2 eggs
30 ml/2 tbsp water
Salt and freshly ground black pepper
15 g/½ oz/1 tbsp butter or margarine
A little chopped fresh parsley

① Break the eggs into a bowl and beat in the water and a little salt and pepper until blended and evenly yellow.

② Heat the butter or margarine in an omelette pan until foaming. Pour in the egg mixture. Cook, lifting and stirring gently, until the base is golden brown and the mixture is still slightly creamy on top.

③ Hold the pan over a warm plate and tilt it slightly. Flip a third of the omelette over the centre third, then flip the folded two-thirds over the final third as you slide it out on to the plate. Sprinkle with parsley and serve straight away.

PREPARATION TIME: 2–3 MINUTES
COOKING TIME: 3–4 MINUTES

Variations

Cheese: At step 2, sprinkle the omelette with 25 g/1 oz/ ¼ cup grated Cheddar cheese when the omelette is half-cooked.

Spinach: Thaw 100 g/4 oz frozen chopped spinach. Squeeze it thoroughly to remove excess moisture. Add to the eggs when beating (step 1). Sprinkle the omelette with a little freshly grated Parmesan cheese instead of chopped parsley.

Mushroom: Cook 3–4 sliced button mushrooms in 30 ml/ 2 tbsp water until soft, then boil rapidly to evaporate the water. Spoon over the half-cooked omelette at step 2.

Chicken or ham: Add a small handful of chopped, cooked chicken or ham to the beaten eggs before cooking.

Prawn: Thaw a small handful of frozen cooked, peeled prawns (shrimp). Drain on kitchen paper (paper towels) and scatter over the half-cooked omelette. Sprinkle with a few drops of Worcestershire and Tabasco sauces.

Eggs in Mushrooms
SERVES 4

4 very large open-cup mushrooms
1 large tomato
Salt and freshly ground black pepper
150 ml/¼ pt/⅔ cup water
4 small eggs
15 ml/1 tbsp chopped fresh parsley
To serve:
Slices of toast, cut into triangles

① Peel the mushrooms and cut off the stalks. Cut the top and base off the tomato and then cut it into four slices.

② Put the mushrooms in a large frying pan (skillet), gill-sides up. Season with salt and pepper and lay a slice of tomato on top of each.

③ Pour the water around. Bring to the boil, turn down the heat to fairly low, cover with a lid or foil and cook gently for 4 minutes.

④ Break one of the eggs into a cup and slide into one of the mushroom cups. Repeat with the remaining eggs.

⑤ Re-cover and poach for 2–4 minutes or until the eggs are cooked to your liking.

⑥ Carefully transfer to warm plates, sprinkle with the parsley and serve with toast triangles.

PREPARATION TIME: 5 MINUTES
COOKING TIME: 6–8 MINUTES

Lower-fat Fry-up
SERVES 4

It is vital you use a non-stick pan for this recipe.

8 lean rashers (slices) of back bacon, rinded
2 slices of bread
15 ml/1 tbsp sunflower oil
2 tomatoes, halved
4 eggs

① Heat the frying pan (skillet) and add the bacon rashers. Cook for about 2 minutes on each side until golden. Transfer to a plate and keep warm in a low oven.

② Brush the bread on both sides with half the oil. Cut the bread into halves. Reheat the pan, add the bread and the tomatoes and cook for about 2 minutes on each side until golden brown. Transfer to the oven.

③ Add the remaining oil to the pan. Swirl the pan so it coats the base and reheat. Break in the eggs and cook to your liking (use a low heat if you like them soft, a higher heat if you like the edges of your eggs crisp).

④ Arrange the bacon, bread and tomatoes on warm plates, then slide an egg on top of each. Serve straight away.

PREPARATION TIME: 5 MINUTES
COOKING TIME: 10–12 MINUTES

Starters

*A*ll of these starters can be prepared in advance, then just cooked at the last minute before you eat, or cooked, then chilled. Either way, there is very little effort involved. Most of the sauces and dips benefit from being made in advance and chilled for a while to allow the flavours to develop.

Fried Goats' Cheese with Honeyed Walnut Dressing
SERVES 4

2 x 4½ oz/120 g cylinder-shaped goats' cheeses
30 ml/2 tbsp plain (all-purpose) flour
1 egg, beaten
50 g/2 oz/1 cup fresh white breadcrumbs
25 g/1 oz/¼ cup walnut pieces, finely chopped
2 spring onions (scallions), finely chopped
30 ml/2 tbsp clear honey
60 ml/4 tbsp olive oil
30 ml/2 tbsp cider vinegar
Salt and freshly ground black pepper
Sunflower oil, for cooking
100 g/4 oz mixed salad leaves
To serve:
French bread

① Slice each cheese into six rounds. Dip in the flour, then the beaten egg, then the breadcrumbs, to coat completely. Chill until ready to cook.

② Mix the walnuts with the spring onions, honey, olive oil and vinegar. Season to taste with salt and pepper.

③ Heat enough oil to cover the base of a frying pan (skillet). Fry (sauté) the cheese rounds for 1 minute on each side until golden brown. Drain on kitchen paper (paper towels).

④ Pile the salad leaves on plates and spoon the dressing over. Arrange the cheese rounds on top and serve straight away with French bread.

PREPARATION TIME: 10 MINUTES
COOKING TIME: 2 MINUTES

Whiting Goujons with Green Chilli and Avocado Dip

SERVES 6

1 large ripe avocado
15 ml/1 tbsp lemon juice
30 ml/2 tbsp mayonnaise
90 ml/6 tbsp sunflower oil
1 green chilli, seeded and finely chopped
5 ml/1 tsp Worcestershire sauce
2.5 cm/1 in piece of cucumber, finely chopped
Salt and freshly ground black pepper
450 g/1 lb whiting fillets, skinned
30 ml/2 tbsp cornflour (cornstarch)
2 eggs, beaten
100 g/4 oz/2 cups fresh white breadcrumbs
Groundnut (peanut) or corn oil, for deep-frying
Wedges of lemon

① Halve the avocado, remove the stone (pit) and scoop the flesh into a bowl. Add the lemon juice and mash thoroughly with a fork.

② Beat in the mayonnaise, then gradually add the sunflower oil, beating well after each addition until smooth. Stir in the chilli, Worcestershire sauce and cucumber and season to taste with salt and pepper. Cover with clingfilm (plastic wrap) and chill until ready to serve.

③ Dip the fish pieces in the cornflour, seasoned with a little salt and pepper. Put the eggs in one shallow dish and the breadcrumbs in another. Dip the fish in the egg, then the breadcrumbs, to coat completely.

④ Pour about 2 cm/¾ in oil into a large frying pan (skillet) and heat until a cube of day-old bread browns in 30 seconds. Cook the fish in batches for about 2 minutes until crisp and golden brown.

⑤ Remove with a draining spoon and drain on kitchen paper (paper towels). Keep warm while cooking the remainder.

⑥ Spoon the dip into small individual pots. Pile the fish on warm plates with a small pot of the dip to one side. Garnish with wedges of lemon and serve straight away.

PREPARATION TIME: 12 MINUTES
COOKING TIME: 6 MINUTES (2 MINUTES PER BATCH)

Camembert and Bacon Stir-fry
SERVES 4

---

100 g/4 oz Camembert, cut into small dice
60 ml/4 tbsp sunflower oil
100 g/4 oz lardons
1 onion, thinly sliced
350 g/12 oz ready-prepared stir-fry vegetables with beansprouts
30 ml/2 tbsp soy sauce
15 ml/1 tbsp balsamic vinegar
4 large crisp lettuce leaves
To serve:
French bread

---

① Put the diced cheese in the fridge until ready to use.

② Heat the oil in a large frying pan (skillet). Add the lardons and onion and fry (sauté), stirring, for 4 minutes until golden.

③ Add the stir-fry vegetables and cook, stirring and tossing, for 4 minutes.

④ Add the cheese, soy sauce and balsamic vinegar and toss for 30 seconds until the cheese is melting.

⑤ Put the lettuce leaves on four small plates. Spoon the stir-fry on top and serve straight away with French bread.

PREPARATION TIME: 3 MINUTES
COOKING TIME: 8–9 MINUTES

Garlic Squid with Tabasco Sauce
SERVES 4

This is also good made with raw, peeled tiger prawns (jumbo shrimp). You will need 24 prawns for four people.

---

12 baby squid tubes, cleaned
50 g/2 oz/¼ cup unsalted (sweet) butter
60 ml/4 tbsp olive oil
1 onion, finely chopped
1 large garlic clove, crushed
15 ml/1 tbsp chopped fresh coriander (cilantro)
45 ml/3 tbsp chopped fresh parsley
2.5 ml/½ tsp Tabasco sauce
Salt and freshly ground black pepper
Juice of ½ lemon
Wedges of lemon
To serve:
Crusty bread

---

① Cut the squid tubes into rings.

② Melt the butter with the oil in a frying pan (skillet) until foaming.

③ Add the onion and garlic and cook gently for 2 minutes until softened but not browned.

④ Add the squid and cook, stirring, for 3 minutes. Add the coriander, 15 ml/1 tbsp of the parsley, the Tabasco sauce, a good pinch of salt, lots of pepper and the lemon juice. Stir, then cover, turn down the heat and cook gently for 10 minutes until the squid is really tender.

⑤ Spoon into warm, shallow dishes, garnish with wedges of lemon and sprinkle with the remaining chopped parsley. Serve straight away with lots of crusty bread.

PREPARATION TIME: 6 MINUTES
COOKING TIME: 15 MINUTES

Mushroom Pâté
SERVES 4–6

25 g/1 oz/2 tbsp butter
1 onion, finely chopped
350 g/12 oz flat mushrooms, peeled and finely chopped
15 ml/1 tbsp dry white wine
5 ml/1 tsp lemon juice
Salt and freshly ground black pepper
225 g/8 oz/1 cup medium-fat soft cheese
15 ml/1 tbsp chopped fresh parsley
15 ml/1 tbsp snipped fresh chives
Twists of lemon
A few sprigs of fresh parsley
To serve:
Hot French bread

① Heat the butter in a frying pan (skillet). Add the onion and fry (sauté), stirring, for 3 minutes until lightly golden.

② Add the mushrooms and wine and cook, stirring, until no liquid remains.

③ Remove from the heat and stir in the lemon juice and some seasoning. Tip into a bowl and leave to cool.

④ When cold, add the cheese and herbs and beat well until thoroughly blended.

⑤ Pack the pâté into small pots and chill for several hours until fairly firm.

⑥ Garnish each pot with a twist of lemon and a sprig of parsley and serve with hot French bread.

PREPARATION TIME: 10 MINUTES PLUS CHILLING
COOKING TIME: 7 MINUTES

Whitebait with Lemon and Tarragon

SERVES 4

450 g/1 lb whitebait
45 ml/3 tbsp plain (all-purpose) flour
Finely grated rind of 1 lemon
30 ml/2 tbsp chopped fresh tarragon
Salt and freshly ground black pepper
Groundnut (peanut) or corn oil, for deep-frying
Wedges of lemon
A few sprigs of fresh tarragon
To serve:
Brown bread and butter

① Spread the whitebait out on kitchen paper (paper towels) and pick them over to remove any weed and broken bits of fish. Do not wash.

② Mix the flour with the lemon rind, chopped tarragon and a little salt and pepper in a shallow dish. Toss the whitebait in this to coat completely.

③ Pour about 2 cm/¾ in oil into a large frying pan (skillet) and heat until a cube of day-old bread browns in 30 seconds. Deep-fry the fish in small batches for about 3 minutes until golden and crisp. Remove with a draining spoon, drain on kitchen paper and keep warm in a low oven while cooking the remainder.

④ Pile on warm plates, garnish with wedges of lemon and sprigs of tarragon and serve straight away with brown bread and butter.

PREPARATION TIME: 5 MINUTES
COOKING TIME: 12 MINUTES (3 MINUTES PER BATCH)

King Prawns in Blankets with Sweet Chilli Sauce

SERVES 4

These are lovely hot, but can be served cold if necessary.

225 g/8 oz/1 small can of chopped tomatoes, drained
1 red chilli, seeded and finely chopped
30 ml/2 tbsp tomato ketchup (catsup)
10 ml/2 tsp balsamic vinegar
10 ml/2 tsp clear honey
Salt and freshly ground black pepper
6 sheets of filo pastry (paste)
24 raw peeled tiger prawns (jumbo shrimp), tails left on
Sunflower or corn oil, for cooking
A few sprigs of fresh parsley

① Mix the tomatoes, chilli, ketchup, vinegar and honey together and season to taste with salt and pepper. Spoon into small pots and chill until ready to serve.

② Fold each piece of pastry in half, then cut, starting from the fold, into four strips. Brush all over with water.

③ Lay a prawn on each strip with the end of the tail projecting over the edge of the pastry. Wrap the pastry round the prawn to form little wedge-shaped parcels with a tiny end of tail sticking out. Press the pastry together to seal.

④ Heat enough oil to cover the base of a frying pan (skillet) and cook the prawn parcels in batches for about 1 minute on each side until crisp and golden. Drain each batch on kitchen paper (paper towels) and keep warm in a low oven while cooking the remainder.

⑤ Put on individual plates with a bowl of sauce on each and garnish with sprigs of parsley. Serve hot.

PREPARATION TIME: 15 MINUTES
COOKING TIME: 6–8 MINUTES (2 MINUTES PER BATCH)

Melting Aubergine Slices
SERVES 4

For a less fattening version, brush the slices of aubergine (eggplant) with just a little oil and omit the flour.

1 large aubergine
45 ml/3 tbsp plain (all-purpose) flour
Salt and freshly ground black pepper
75 ml/5 tbsp olive oil
150 ml/¼ pt/⅔ cup passata (sieved tomatoes)
15 ml/1 tbsp chopped fresh basil
100 g/4 oz Mozzarella cheese, sliced
A few sprigs of fresh basil
To serve:
Ciabatta bread

① Trim the top off the aubergine, then cut lengthways into four thick slices.

② Mix the flour with a little salt and pepper and use to coat the aubergine slices.

③ Heat 45 ml/3 tbsp of the oil in a large frying pan (skillet). Fry (sauté) the aubergine slices on one side for about 3 minutes until golden. Turn over, add the remaining oil to the pan and fry for 2 minutes. Remove the aubergine from the pan.

④ Add the passata and basil to the pan and season lightly. Bring to the boil. Put the aubergine slices back in the pan and top with the cheese. Cover with a lid or foil and cook for 2 minutes.

⑤ Carefully transfer the cheese-topped aubergine to warm plates and spoon the passata around. Garnish with sprigs of basil and serve straight away with ciabatta bread.

PREPARATION TIME: 5 MINUTES
COOKING TIME: 8 MINUTES

Crunchy Crumbed Mushrooms with Aioli

SERVES 4

---

150 ml/¼ pt/⅔ cup mayonnaise
60 ml/4 tbsp crème fraîche
2 garlic cloves, crushed
15 ml/1 tbsp chopped fresh parsley
Salt and freshly ground black pepper
85 g/3½ oz/1 small packet of country-style stuffing mix
2 eggs
225 g/8 oz small button mushrooms
Sunflower oil, for cooking
Wedges of lemon
A few sprigs of fresh parsley

---

① To make the aioli, mix the mayonnaise, crème fraîche, garlic and parsley together and season to taste. Spoon the mixture into a serving dish, cover with clingfilm (plastic wrap) and chill until ready to serve.

② Tip the stuffing mix on to a plate. Beat the eggs on a separate plate.

③ Wipe the mushrooms with damp kitchen paper (paper towels), then trim the stalks if necessary.

④ Dip the mushrooms in the egg, then the stuffing mix, to coat completely.

⑤ Heat enough oil to cover the base of a large frying pan (skillet). Add half the mushrooms and fry (sauté) for about 3–4 minutes until golden, turning once or twice. Drain on kitchen paper. Keep warm in a low oven while cooking the remainder.

⑥ Pile on warm plates, garnish with lemon and parsley and serve with the aioli.

PREPARATION TIME: 15 MINUTES
COOKING TIME: 6–8 MINUTES

Blinis with Smoked Mackerel

SERVES 4

Blinis are usually made with yeast and take a while to make but these take only a few minutes.

2 smoked mackerel fillets
150 ml/¼ pt/⅔ cup double (heavy) cream
30 ml/2 tbsp horseradish relish
Salt and freshly ground black pepper
100 g/4 oz/1 cup self-raising (self-rising) flour
2 eggs, separated
300 ml/½ pt/1¼ cups milk
Sunflower oil, for cooking
1 bunch of spring onions (scallions), finely chopped
Wedges of lemon

① Remove the skin from the fish and flake the flesh using two forks. Place in a container with a lid. Seal and store in the fridge until ready to serve.

② Whip the cream with the horseradish until peaking. Season to taste.

③ Mix the flour and a pinch of salt in a bowl. Add the egg yolks and half the milk and beat well until smooth. Beat in the remaining milk.

④ Whisk the egg whites until stiff and fold into the batter mixture with a metal spoon.

⑤ Heat a little oil in a large frying pan (skillet) and pour off the excess. Add enough of the batter mixture to make two 10 cm/4 in rounds in the pan. Cook until they are golden underneath and bubbles are rising to the surface. Flip over and cook the other sides until golden. Slide on to a napkin on a plate, wrap and keep warm over a pan of gently simmering water. Repeat until all the batter is used (it should make 12 blinis).

⑥ Arrange three blinis on each of four plates with a pile of mackerel. Add a spoonful of horseradish cream and a little chopped spring onion and serve, garnished with wedges of lemon.

PREPARATION TIME: 10 MINUTES
COOKING TIME: ABOUT 15 MINUTES (2–3 MINUTES PER BATCH)

Warm Chicken Liver and Blueberry Salad
SERVES 4

225 g/8 oz chicken livers, trimmed
90 ml/6 tbsp olive oil
1 red onion, finely chopped
50 g/2 oz lambs' tongue lettuce
100 g/4 oz blueberries
45 ml/3 tbsp sherry vinegar
15 ml/1 tbsp blackcurrant cordial
Salt and freshly ground black pepper
30 ml/2 tbsp chopped fresh parsley

① Cut each chicken liver into two or three pieces.

② Heat half the oil in a frying pan (skillet). Add the onion and fry (sauté), stirring, for 2 minutes. Add the chicken livers and continue to fry for a further 4 minutes until just cooked but still pink and tender. Season lightly.

③ Meanwhile, pile the lettuce on four plates. Lift the chicken livers and onion out of the pan with a draining spoon and scatter on the leaves.

④ Quickly add the remaining oil to the pan with the blueberries, vinegar, blackcurrant cordial and a little salt and pepper. Bring to the boil, stirring.

⑤ Spoon immediately over the salad. Sprinkle with parsley and serve straight away.

PREPARATION TIME: 8 MINUTES
COOKING TIME: 7 MINUTES

Crispy Potato Skins with Cooling Cucumber Dip

SERVES 4

Use the scooped-out potato for any recipe that calls for cooked, leftover potato.

8 medium potatoes, scrubbed
10 cm/4 in piece of cucumber, grated
150 ml/¼ pt/⅔ cup Greek-style yoghurt
1 spring onion (scallion), finely chopped
5 ml/1 tsp dried dill (dill weed)
Salt and freshly ground black pepper
Groundnut (peanut) or corn oil, for deep-frying

① Prick the potatoes and bake in the oven at 200°C/400°F/gas mark 6 (fan oven 180°C) for about 1 hour. Alternatively, wrap in kitchen paper (paper towels) and cook in the microwave on Full Power for about 30 minutes (depending on the output), until soft when squeezed.

② Meanwhile, squeeze the grated cucumber to remove the excess moisture. Mix into the yoghurt with the spring onion, dill and salt and pepper to taste. Chill until ready to serve.

③ Cut the cooked potatoes into halves and scoop out most of the potato, leaving an 8 mm/⅓ in shell. Cut each shell in half lengthways.

④ Pour about 2 cm/¾ in of oil into a large frying pan (skillet) and heat until a cube of day-old bread browns in 30 seconds. Cook the skins, a few at a time, for about 1 minute until really crisp. Remove with a draining spoon and drain on kitchen paper.

⑤ Sprinkle a good pinch of salt over the potato skins. Spoon the chilled yoghurt mixture into small pots and place in the centre of the plates. Pile the potato skins around and serve.

PREPARATION TIME: 1–1¼ HOURS (INCLUDING BAKING POTATOES)
COOKING TIME: 4–5 MINUTES (1 MINUTE PER BATCH)

Fish and Seafood

*A*ll kinds of fish and seafood cook quickly and are ideal for the frying pan (skillet) treatment. This chapter contains a whole selection of colourful, nutritious and spectacular dishes for you to try. Many are great everyday meals, others will be perfect to impress your friends and family when entertaining. Always remember, don't overcook fish or it will become dry.

Tuna Steaks with Creamy Salsa
SERVES 4

If you like your tuna pink in the middle, cook for only 2 minutes on each side. If you don't have steak seasoning, use plenty of freshly ground black pepper and a little salt instead.

4 tuna steaks
A little olive oil
5 ml/1 tsp steak seasoning
For the salsa:
175 ml/6 fl oz/¾ cup ready-made tomato pasta sauce
90 ml/6 tbsp crème fraîche
60 ml/4 tbsp dry white wine
30 ml/2 tbsp tomato ketchup (catsup)
A few sprigs of fresh parsley
To serve:
Mediterranean Vegetables (see page 119)
   and ciabatta bread

① Brush the tuna steaks with oil on both sides, then sprinkle with the steak seasoning.

② Mix the salsa ingredients together in a bowl.

③ Heat a heavy-based, non-stick frying pan (skillet) or griddle. When hot, add the tuna and cook for about 3–4 minutes on each side until just cooked through. Transfer to a plate and keep warm.

④ Add the salsa to the pan and heat, stirring, until hot through.

⑤ Spoon the salsa on to warm plates and top each with a tuna steak. Garnish with a sprig of parsley and serve hot with Mediterranean Vegetables and ciabatta bread.

PREPARATION TIME: 5 MINUTES
COOKING TIME: 6–8 MINUTES

Trout with Garlic, Herbs and Almonds
SERVES 4

4 trout, cleaned
Salt and freshly ground black pepper
50 g/2 oz/¼ cup butter or margarine
30 ml/2 tbsp sunflower oil
1 large garlic clove, crushed
50 g/2 oz/½ cup flaked (slivered) almonds
30 ml/2 tbsp chopped fresh parsley
30 ml/2 tbsp chopped fresh basil
15 ml/1 tbsp lemon or lime juice
Wedges of lemon or lime
A few sprigs of fresh parsley
To serve:
New potatoes and mangetout (snow peas)

① Wipe the fish inside and out with kitchen paper (paper towels). Cut off the heads, if liked. Make several slashes on each side and season with salt and pepper.

② Heat the butter or margarine with the oil in a large frying pan (skillet). When foaming, add the garlic and stir for 30 seconds. Add the fish and cook for 5 minutes on each side until cooked through. Transfer to warm plates and keep warm.

③ Add the almonds to the pan and stir for 1 minute until lightly golden. Add the herbs and lemon or lime juice. Stir and spoon over the fish immediately.

④ Garnish with wedges of lemon or lime and sprigs of parsley and serve with new potatoes and mangetout.

PREPARATION TIME: 5 MINUTES
COOKING TIME: 12 MINUTES

Ginger Soy Mackerel with Crispy Seaweed

SERVES 4

4 small mackerel, cleaned
40 ml/8 tsp slivered sweet pickled ginger
30 ml/2 tbsp soy sauce
30 ml/2 tbsp sunflower oil
Groundnut (peanut) or corn oil, for cooking
350 g/12 oz spring (collard) greens, finely shredded
30 ml/2 tbsp toasted sesame seeds
A few drops of balsamic vinegar
To serve:
Chinese egg noodles, sprinkled with sesame oil

① Wipe the mackerel inside and out and make several slashes on each side. Cut off the heads. Spoon 10 ml/2 tsp of the ginger into the body cavity of each fish and spread out.

② Whisk the soy sauce and sunflower oil in a large, shallow dish. Lay the fish in the dish and turn over in the mixture to coat. Leave to marinate in the fridge while you cook the greens.

④ Pour about 2 cm/¾ in cooking oil into a deep frying pan (skillet) and heat until a cube of day-old bread browns in 30 seconds. Fry (sauté) the shredded greens in batches for about 2 minutes until crispy. Remove with a draining spoon and drain on kitchen paper (paper towels) while cooking the remainder. Keep warm.

⑤ Pour off the hot oil, then heat the pan again and add the mackerel. Fry for about 5 minutes on each side until golden and cooked through.

⑦ Sprinkle the 'seaweed' with sesame seeds and pile on four warm plates. Lay a mackerel to one side of each plate and sprinkle with a few drops of balsamic vinegar. Serve with hot Chinese egg noodles, sprinkled with sesame oil.

PREPARATION AND TIME: 8 MINUTES
COOKING TIME: 15–20 MINUTES

Rustic Swordfish Steaks with Mushrooms and New Potatoes

SERVES 4

---

50 g/2 oz/¼ cup butter
60 ml/4 tbsp olive oil
350 g/12 oz baby new potatoes, scrubbed
4 swordfish steaks
100 g/4 oz button mushrooms
Juice of ½ lemon
Salt and freshly ground black pepper
30 ml/2 tbsp chopped fresh parsley
2 garlic cloves, finely chopped
To serve:
A green salad

---

① Heat 15 g/½ oz/1 tbsp of the butter and 15 ml/1 tbsp of the oil in a large frying pan (skillet). Add the potatoes and fry (sauté), stirring, until browned all over. Cover the pan with a lid, reduce the heat and cook for about 10 minutes until tender, shaking the pan occasionally.

② Remove from the pan with a draining spoon. Heat the remaining butter and oil in the pan, then add the fish and brown on both sides.

③ Return the potatoes to the pan and add the mushrooms. Sprinkle with the lemon juice, some salt and pepper, the parsley and garlic. Cover with a lid and cook gently for 5 minutes.

④ Serve straight from the pan with a green salad.

PREPARATION TIME: 5 MINUTES
COOKING TIME: 20 MINUTES

Thai-style Crab Cakes with Green Spiced Mayonnaise

SERVES 4

1 red (bell) pepper
175 ml/6 fl oz/¾ cup mayonnaise
1 stalk of lemon grass, finely chopped
1 small red onion, very finely chopped `
2 x 170 g/6 oz/small cans of white crabmeat, drained
100 g/4 oz/2 cups fresh white breadcrumbs
15 ml/1 tbsp chopped fresh coriander (cilantro)
15 ml/1 tbsp chopped fresh parsley
1.5 ml/¼ tsp chilli powder
Salt and freshly ground black pepper
A little milk, if necessary
15 ml/1 tbsp green curry paste
15 ml/1 tbsp lemon juice
Oil, for shallow-frying
Wedges of lemon
A few sprigs of fresh coriander
To serve:
A beansprout and green pepper salad

① Put the red pepper in a bowl and cover with boiling water. Leave to stand for 5 minutes, then drain, rinse with cold water and drain again. Halve, remove the core and seeds and pull off the skin. Finely chop and return to the bowl.

② Add 90 ml/6 tbsp of the mayonnaise, the lemon grass, onion, crab, breadcrumbs, herbs and chilli powder. Mix together thoroughly and season to taste with salt and pepper. Add a little milk to moisten if necessary, and shape the mixture into eight small cakes. Chill until ready to cook.

③ Mix the remaining mayonnaise with the green curry paste and sharpen with lemon juice.

④ Heat the oil in a frying pan (skillet) and fry (sauté) the cakes in two batches for 2–3 minutes on each side until golden. Drain on kitchen paper (paper towels).

⑤ Transfer to warm plates, garnish with wedges of lemon and sprigs of coriander. Spoon the green mayonnaise to one side and serve with a beansprout and pepper salad.

PREPARATION TIME: 15 MINUTES
COOKING TIME: 8–12 MINUTES

Crunchy-topped Cod Supper
SERVES 4

Use any chunky white fish for this dish.

700 g/1½ lb cod fillet, cut into 4 equal pieces
Salt and freshly ground black pepper
A few drops of Worcestershire sauce
30 ml/2 tbsp olive oil
4 tomatoes, sliced
100 g/4 oz/1 cup Cheddar cheese, grated
25 g/1 oz/½ cup cornflakes, crushed
To serve:
Creamed potatoes and peas

① Wipe the fish. Season with salt and pepper and sprinkle on both sides with a few drops of Worcestershire sauce.

② Heat the oil in a frying pan (skillet) and cook the fish, skin-side up, for 2 minutes. Carefully turn over.

③ Lay the tomato slices on top of each fish fillet. Mix the cheese and cornflakes together and pile on top of each. Cover with a lid or foil and cook for a further 3–5 minutes until the cheese melts and bubbles. Alternatively, cook uncovered for 2 minutes, then flash the pan under a preheated grill (broiler) until the top is golden and bubbling.

④ Serve straight from the pan with creamed potatoes and peas.

PREPARATION TIME: 5 MINUTES
COOKING TIME: 5–7 MINUTES

Pan-roasted Monkfish with Bacon

SERVES 4

Monkfish is expensive but it has a wonderful meaty texture. It makes the perfect special occasion dish, stuffed with exotic mushrooms and wrapped in bacon. For extra elegance, toss a few cooked, peeled prawns (shrimp) into the pan with the lemon juice after cooking the fish.

50 g/2 oz chanterelle mushrooms, finely chopped
50 g/2 oz/¼ cup butter, softened
30 ml/2 tbsp chopped fresh parsley
Finely grated rind and juice of ½ lemon
Salt and freshly ground black pepper
1 monkfish tail, about 450 g/1 lb
6 rashers (slices) of smoked streaky bacon, rinded
30 ml/2 tbsp olive oil
A few sprigs of fresh parsley
Wedges of lemon
To serve:
New potatoes and a green salad

① Mash the mushrooms with the butter. Work in the parsley and lemon rind. Season the mixture with a pinch of salt and lots of pepper.

② Cut the central bone out of the fish, taking care not to cut the fish right through. Spoon the mushroom mixture into the slit left by the bone and spread out. Re-shape the fish and press the sides firmly together.

③ Stretch the bacon rashers with the back of a knife and wrap tightly round the fish to cover it completely. Secure any loose ends with cocktail sticks (toothpicks).

④ Heat the oil in a frying pan (skillet). Add the fish and brown for 2 minutes on each side. Turn down the heat to moderate and cover the pan with a lid or foil. Cook for a further 10 minutes, turning once.

⑤ Transfer to a board. Remove the cocktail sticks.

⑥ Add the lemon juice to the pan and bring to the boil. Season to taste if necessary.

⑦ Cut the fish into thick slices and arrange on warm plates. Spoon the pan juices over and garnish with sprigs of parsley and wedges of lemon. Serve with new potatoes and a green salad.

PREPARATION TIME: 20 MINUTES
COOKING TIME: 15 MINUTES

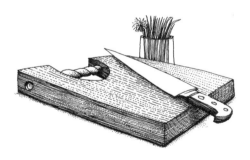

Battered Fish with Giant Chips

SERVES 4

If you love good old fish 'n' chips but fancy a bit of a change, this should do the trick. Cod is my favourite fish for this recipe but you can use haddock or huss if you prefer.

425 g/15 oz/1 large can of garden peas
4 large potatoes, scrubbed
Sunflower oil, for cooking
100 g/4 oz/1 cup self-raising (self-rising) flour
A good pinch of salt
150 ml/¼ pt/⅔ cup cold water
700 g/1½ lb cod fillet, cut into 4 equal pieces
To serve:
Vinegar and tomato ketchup (catsup)

① Purée the peas and their liquid in a blender or food processor, or rub through a sieve (strainer). Place in a saucepan.

② Cut each potato lengthways into six slices. Pat them dry on kitchen paper (paper towels).

③ Heat enough oil to cover the base of a large frying pan (skillet). Add the potato slices and fry (sauté) in batches for about 3 minutes on each side until golden brown and tender. Remove from the pan with a draining spoon. Drain on kitchen paper, then keep warm in a low oven.

④ Whisk the flour, salt and water together. Add a little more oil and reheat. Dip the fish in the batter, then fry in the hot oil for about 5 minutes until crisp, golden and cooked through, turning once. Drain on kitchen paper.

⑤ Meanwhile, heat the pea purée.

⑥ Spoon the purée on four warm plates. Arrange six potato slices in a fan shape on each plate. Lay a piece of fish at the base of each fan. Serve with vinegar and ketchup.

PREPARATION TIME: 10 MINUTES
COOKING TIME: ABOUT 20 MINUTES

Herrings in Mustard and Oatmeal
SERVES 4

This is a traditional dish with an original twist. Ask your fishmonger to prepare the fish if you aren't sure how to do it. If you have two large pans, you can cook the fish all in one go, with half the butter and oil in each pan.

60 ml/4 tbsp medium oatmeal
5 ml/1 tsp mustard powder
30 ml/2 tbsp chopped fresh parsley
Finely grated rind of ½ orange
4 small herrings, cleaned, heads removed, scaled and boned
Salt and freshly ground black pepper
45 ml/3 tbsp milk
50 g/2 oz/¼ cup butter or margarine
30 ml/2 tbsp sunflower oil
Twists of orange
A few sprigs of fresh parsley
To serve:
New potatoes and peas

① Mix the oatmeal on a plate with the mustard powder, parsley and orange rind.

② Rinse the fish and pat dry on kitchen paper (paper towels).

③ Season the fish with salt and pepper, then dip in the milk, then the oatmeal mixture, to coat completely.

④ Heat the butter or margarine and oil in a large frying pan (skillet). Add two of the fish and fry (sauté) for about 5 minutes on each side until golden brown and cooked through. Drain on kitchen paper and keep warm while cooking the other two fish.

⑤ Garnish with orange twists and sprigs of parsley and serve hot with new potatoes and peas.

PREPARATION TIME: 15 MINUTES
COOKING TIME: 20 MINUTES (10 MINUTES PER BATCH)

Warm Salmon and Rocket Salad with Parmesan

SERVES 4

You can buy Parmesan cheese ready cut into shavings but it's cheaper to buy a block and pare it off with a potato peeler.

2 slices of wholemeal bread
Butter, for spreading
50 g/2 oz rocket leaves
¼ cucumber, cut into small dice
1 green (bell) pepper, cut into small dice
8 cherry tomatoes, halved
25 g/1 oz/¼ cup Parmesan cheese, cut into thin shavings
90 ml/6 tbsp olive oil
4 salmon tail fillets
30 ml/2 tbsp balsamic vinegar
Freshly ground black pepper

① Spread the bread with butter on both sides, then cut into small cubes. Fry (sauté) in a large frying pan (skillet), tossing until golden brown. Remove from the pan with a draining spoon and drain on kitchen paper (paper towels).

② Mix the rocket with the cucumber, pepper and tomatoes and pile on plates. Scatter the shavings of Parmesan and the croûtons over.

③ Heat a little of the oil in the frying pan. Add the salmon fillets, skin-side up, and fry for 1 minute. Turn over and continue to fry for a further 5 minutes until cooked through. Carefully lift on to the salads.

④ Quickly add the remaining oil and the balsamic vinegar to the pan with a good grinding of pepper and stir until bubbling. Spoon over the salads and serve straight away.

PREPARATION TIME: 10 MINUTES
COOKING TIME: 7 MINUTES

Fritto Misto di Mare

SERVES 4–6

*If you like dipping your fish, serve with aioli (see page 47)
or tartare sauce.*

100 g/4 oz/1 cup plain (all-purpose) flour
20 ml/1½ tbsp olive oil
A good pinch of salt
300 ml/½ pt/1¼ cups lukewarm water
1 egg white
Groundnut (peanut) or corn oil, for deep-frying
225 g/8 oz squid rings
225 g/8 oz raw peeled tiger prawns (jumbo shrimp)
225 g/8 oz queen scallops
225 g/8 oz sole fillets, cut into thin strips
Wedges of lemon
A few sprigs of fresh parsley
To serve:
Focaccia bread and a large mixed salad

① Put the flour in a bowl. Add the olive oil and salt, then gradually work in the water until the mixture forms a thick, smooth batter. Whisk the egg white until stiff and fold into the batter with a metal spoon.

② Pour about 2 cm/¾ in oil into a large frying pan (skillet) and heat until a cube of day-old bread browns in 30 seconds.

③ Dip the squid in the batter and lower the coated pieces gently into the hot oil. Cook for about 3–4 minutes until crisp and golden. Remove with a draining spoon, drain on kitchen paper (paper towels), then keep warm in a low oven while you cook the prawns, the scallops and finally the sole fillets. Reheat the oil between batches.

④ Serve the crispy mixed seafood, garnished with wedges of lemon and sprigs of parsley, with focaccia bread and a mixed salad.

PREPARATION TIME: 8 MINUTES
COOKING TIME: 12–16 MINUTES

Golden Seafood Macaroni
SERVES 4

This is a pasta version of a paella. If you don't have any saffron powder, you can use ground turmeric instead.

---

30 ml/2 tbsp olive oil
1 large onion, chopped
1 garlic clove, crushed
350 g/12 oz quick-cook macaroni
1.2 litres/2 pts/5 cups fish, chicken or vegetable stock, made with 2 stock cubes
2.5 ml/½ tsp saffron powder
2.5 ml/½ tsp dried oregano
100 g/4 oz frozen peas
400 g/14 oz mixed seafood cocktail, e.g. tiger prawns (jumbo shrimp), squid, mussels and scallops
Salt and freshly ground black pepper
A little chopped fresh parsley
Wedges of lemon
To serve:
French bread

---

① Heat the oil in a large frying pan (skillet). Add the onion and garlic and cook gently, stirring, for 2 minutes until softened but not browned.

② Add the macaroni and stir until each tube is coated in oil.

③ Add the stock, saffron and oregano and bring to the boil, stirring. Reduce the heat, cover and simmer gently for 10 minutes, stirring once or twice.

④ Add the peas and seafood, stir again, re-cover and cook for a further 10 minutes until the pasta is tender and has absorbed nearly all the liquid. Season to taste with salt and pepper and stir gently again. Sprinkle with the parsley, garnish with wedges of lemon and serve straight from the pan with French bread.

PREPARATION TIME: 5 MINUTES
COOKING TIME: 25 MINUTES

Meat Dishes

*I*t's not unusual to fry (sauté) steaks, chops or chicken breasts in your frying pan (skillet) but your trusty utensil is also great for cooking them in sumptuous sauces too – and it's far quicker than cooking a casserole. Although it means you have to use good-quality, tender cuts, they aren't that much dearer than their tougher counterparts and, because they cook so quickly, you save on time – and fuel costs.

Swiss-style Steak
SERVES 4

30 ml/2 tbsp sunflower oil
1 onion, finely chopped
450 g/1 lb rump steak, cubed
225 g/8 oz small button mushrooms, halved
400 g/14 oz/1 large can of chopped tomatoes
15 ml/1 tbsp tomato purée (paste)
5 ml/1 tsp caster (superfine) sugar
Salt and freshly ground black pepper
2.5 ml/½ tsp dried mixed herbs
30 ml/2 tbsp crème fraîche
15 ml/1 tbsp chopped fresh parsley
To serve:
Rice or noodles and a green salad

① Heat the oil in a large frying pan (skillet). Add the onion and fry (sauté) for 2 minutes.

② Add the steak and continue to fry, stirring, until browned on all sides.

③ Add all the remaining ingredients except the crème fraîche and parsley. Bring to the boil, stirring. Turn down the heat until gently bubbling round the edges. Cover with a lid or foil and cook gently for 10 minutes.

④ Swirl the crème fraîche over the surface, sprinkle with parsley and serve with rice or noodles and a green salad.

PREPARATION TIME: 8 MINUTES
COOKING TIME: 15 MINUTES

Italian-style Meatballs with Pasta

SERVES 4

---

1 onion, very finely chopped
450 g/1 lb lean minced (ground) steak
1 garlic clove, crushed
2.5 ml/½ tsp dried oregano
Salt and freshly ground black pepper
1 egg, beaten
15 ml/1 tbsp olive oil
295 g/10½ oz/1 medium can of condensed tomato soup
225 g/8 oz quick-cook macaroni
30 ml/2 tbsp chopped fresh basil
30 ml/2 tbsp freshly grated Parmesan cheese
To serve:
A cucumber and rocket salad

---

① Mix the onion with the meat, garlic, oregano and some salt and pepper. Add the beaten egg and mix well to bind. Shape into 20 small balls.

② Heat the oil in a large frying pan (skillet). Add the meatballs and brown on all sides for 3–4 minutes. Remove from the pan with a draining spoon. Pour off the fat.

③ Add the can of tomato soup to the pan. Fill the can with water, pour into the soup and stir until well blended. Add a further canful of water. Bring to the boil.

④ Stir in the macaroni, season to taste and bring back to the boil. Turn down the heat until bubbling gently. Cover with a lid or foil and cook for 10 minutes, stirring once or twice.

⑤ Stir in the basil, return the meatballs to the pan and cook gently for a further 10 minutes or until the macaroni is tender and bathed in a rich sauce. Spoon into warm shallow bowls. Sprinkle with Parmesan cheese and serve with a cucumber and rocket salad.

PREPARATION TIME: 10 MINUTES
COOKING TIME: 25–30 MINUTES

Traditional Keema Curry

SERVES 4

*An Indian friend gave this recipe to me over 25 years ago.
He used to make his own curry powder. I cheat and use
ready-made, but it still tastes extremely good!*

30 ml/2 tbsp sunflower oil
2 onions, chopped
450 g/1 lb lean minced (ground) beef
30 ml/2 tbsp medium curry powder
3 garlic cloves, crushed
5 ml/1 tsp finely grated fresh root ginger
300 ml/½ pt/1¼ cups water
15 ml/1 tbsp tomato purée (paste)
A little salt
A few fresh coriander (cilantro) leaves, torn
To serve:
Rice and mango chutney

① Heat the oil in a large frying pan (skillet). Add the onions and fry (sauté) gently, stirring, for 2 minutes until softened but not browned.

② Add the meat and fry, stirring, until it is no longer pink and all the grains are separate.

③ Stir in the curry powder and fry for a further 3 minutes, stirring.

④ Add the garlic, ginger, water, tomato purée and salt to taste. Bring to the boil, stirring, then reduce the heat and simmer gently for 15–20 minutes, stirring from time to time. Taste and add more salt if necessary.

⑤ Sprinkle the coriander leaves over and serve with rice and mango chutney.

PREPARATION TIME: 5 MINUTES
COOKING TIME: 25–30 MINUTES

Spicy Beef Leaves

SERVES 4

If the steak slices are very large, you can use four instead of eight.

30 ml/2 tbsp olive oil
25 g/1 oz/2 tbsp butter or margarine
8 thin slices of frying steak
1 onion, very finely chopped
1 garlic clove, finely chopped
1 red chilli, seeded and finely chopped
60 ml/4 tbsp Worcestershire sauce
15 ml/1 tbsp soy sauce
30 ml/2 tbsp water
20 ml/1½ tbsp fresh lime juice
15 ml/1 tbsp chopped fresh coriander (cilantro)
15 ml/1 tbsp chopped fresh parsley
Salt and freshly ground black pepper
To serve:
Stir-fried Mangetout and Baby Sweetcorn (see page 122)
  and wild rice mix

① Heat the oil and butter or margarine in a large frying pan (skillet). Add the steak and fry (sauté) for 45 seconds to 1 minute on each side until browned and just cooked. Remove to a plate and keep warm in a low oven.

② Add the onion, garlic and chilli to the pan and cook, stirring, for 2 minutes. Stir in the remaining ingredients and allow to bubble for 30 seconds.

③ Put the beef slices on warm plates. Spoon the chilli juices over and serve with Stir-fried Mangetout with Baby Sweetcorn and wild rice mix.

PREPARATION TIME: 5 MINUTES
COOKING TIME: 3–4 MINUTES

Marrakesh Lamb

SERVES 4

This tastes just like a proper Moroccan tagine but takes only a fraction of the time to cook.

250 g/9 oz lamb neck fillets
2.5 ml/½ tsp ground cinnamon
2.5 ml/½ tsp ground ginger
2.5 ml/½ tsp ground cumin
1.5 ml/¼ tsp salt
1 garlic clove, crushed
Freshly ground black pepper
12 button (pearl) onions
45 ml/3 tbsp olive oil
2 courgettes (zucchini), sliced
1 orange (bell) pepper, diced
100 g/4 oz/⅔ cup ready-to-eat dried apricots, halved
450 ml/¾ pt/2 cups lamb or vegetable stock, made with
 1 stock cube
225 g/8 oz/1⅓ cups couscous
45 ml/3 tbsp tomato purée (paste)
10 ml/2 tsp clear honey
60 ml/4 tbsp soured (dairy sour) cream
A small handful of fresh coriander (cilantro) leaves, torn

① Cut the lamb into slices 5 mm/¼ in thick. Mix the spices in a bowl with the salt, garlic and some pepper. Add the lamb and toss with your hands to coat the meat completely in the mixture. Leave to stand.

② Put the onions in a large frying pan (skillet) and cover with boiling water. Bring back to the boil, cook for 5 minutes, then tip into a colander to drain.

③ Heat 15 ml/1 tbsp of the oil in the pan. Add the courgettes and pepper and cook, stirring, for 3 minutes. Remove from the pan with a draining spoon.

④ Heat the remaining oil in the pan. Add the lamb and brown all over, stirring. Return the onions, courgettes and pepper to the pan with the apricots and stock. Bring back to the boil, cover with foil or a lid and simmer for 10 minutes until tender.

⑤ Put the couscous in a bowl. Add 600 ml/1 pt/2½ cups boiling water, stir, cover and put in the low oven for 5 minutes until fluffy and all the liquid is absorbed.

⑥ Using a draining spoon, transfer the cooked meat and vegetables to a dish and keep warm in the oven.

⑦ Stir the tomato purée and honey into the pan and bring to the boil, stirring. Taste and re-season if necessary. Return the meat and vegetables to the sauce.

⑧ Fluff up the couscous and pile on warm plates. Top with the lamb mixture and add a spoonful of soured cream to each. Garnish with torn coriander leaves and serve.

PREPARATION TIME: 15 MINUTES
COOKING TIME: 20–25 MINUTES

Lamb Steaks in Mint Jus

SERVES 4

To make the potato and parsnip mash, simply boil potatoes with one or two parsnips in lightly salted water until tender. Mash with a knob of butter or margarine and a splash of milk, and season to taste.

---

4 lamb leg steaks
Salt and freshly ground black pepper
30 ml/2 tbsp olive oil
15 ml/1 tbsp cornflour (cornstarch)
30 ml/2 tbsp water
300 ml/½ pt/1¼ cups lamb or chicken stock, made with
  1 stock cube
30 ml/2 tbsp mint sauce
2.5 ml/½ tsp caster (superfine) sugar
To serve:
Potato and parsnip mash (see above), carrots and peas

---

① Season the lamb with salt and pepper.

② Heat the oil in a large frying pan (skillet). Add the lamb and cook for 3–4 minutes on each side until browned and just cooked through. Do not overcook. Transfer to a plate and keep warm in a low oven.

③ Remove the pan from the heat. Blend the cornflour with the water and stir into the juices in the pan. Quickly blend in the stock and stir until smooth. Return to the heat and bring to the boil, stirring. Stir in the mint sauce and sugar and season to taste with salt and pepper. Cook for a further 1 minute.

④ Arrange the lamb steaks on warm plates and spoon the mint jus over. Serve with parsnip and potato mash, carrots and peas.

PREPARATION TIME: 2 MINUTES
COOKING TIME: 8–10 MINUTES

Herb and Almond Crusted Lamb Cutlets
SERVES 4

These are also delicious served cold for a picnic.

8 lamb cutlets
85 g/3½ oz/1 small packet of parsley, thyme and lemon
  stuffing mix
30 ml/2 tbsp chopped almonds
Salt and freshly ground black pepper
2 eggs
45 ml/3 tbsp sunflower oil
Wedges of lemon
A few sprigs of fresh parsley
To serve:
Pan Dauphinoise (see page 109) and French (green) beans

① Wipe the cutlets and trim off any excess fat.

② Mix the stuffing with the almonds on a plate and season with salt and pepper. Beat the eggs on another plate.

③ Dip the cutlets in the egg, then the stuffing mix, to coat completely.

④ Heat the oil in a large frying pan (skillet). Fry (sauté) the cutlets for 4 minutes on each side until golden and slightly pink in the centre. If you like your lamb well done, cook over a moderate heat for about 2 minutes more.

⑤ Drain the lamb on kitchen paper (paper towels), transfer to warm plates, garnish with wedges of lemon and sprigs of parsley and serve with Pan Dauphinoise and French beans.

PREPARATION TIME: 8 MINUTES
COOKING TIME: 8–10 MINUTES

One-pan Moussaka

SERVES 4

1 aubergine (eggplant), sliced
30 ml/2 tbsp olive oil
120 ml/4 fl oz/½ cup water
1 onion, chopped
350 g/12 oz minced (ground) lamb
1 garlic clove, crushed
1.5 ml/¼ tsp ground cinnamon
Salt and freshly ground black pepper
2.5 ml/½ tsp dried oregano
400 g/14 oz/1 large can of chopped tomatoes
2 eggs
200 g/7 oz/scant 1 cup medium-fat soft cheese
30 ml/2 tbsp milk
To serve:
A mixed salad

① Toss the aubergine slices in the oil. Heat a large frying pan (skillet) and fry (sauté) the aubergine slices, turning occasionally, for 1 minute. Add the water and cook for a further 2–3 minutes until the water has been absorbed and the aubergines are soft. Remove from the pan and reserve.

② Add the onion, lamb and garlic to the pan and fry, stirring, until the lamb is no longer pink and all the grains are separate.

③ Add the cinnamon, salt and pepper to taste, the oregano and tomatoes. Cook, stirring occasionally, for 5 minutes. Turn off the heat.

④ Lay the aubergine slices over the top.

⑤ Beat the eggs, cheese and milk together with a little salt and pepper and spoon over the top. Cover with foil or a lid and cook over a gentle heat for 12–15 minutes until the top is set. Serve straight from the pan with a mixed salad.

PREPARATION TIME: 20 MINUTES
COOKING TIME: 12–15 MINUTES

Sweet Spiced Chicken Kiev

SERVES 4

50 g/2 oz/¼ cup butter, softened
5 ml/1 tsp ground cumin
10 ml/2 tsp paprika
1 garlic clove, crushed
15 ml/1 tbsp chopped fresh coriander (cilantro)
Freshly ground black pepper
4 skinless chicken breasts
2 eggs
100 g/4 oz/2 cups fresh wholemeal breadcrumbs
Sunflower or corn oil, for shallow-frying
Wedges of lemon
A few sprigs of fresh coriander
To serve:
Sauté Potatoes (see page 107) and broccoli

① Mash the butter with the cumin, paprika, garlic and chopped coriander. Season well with pepper.

② Make a slit in the side of each chicken breast. Push the flavoured butter inside, making sure the slit sides of the chicken cover the butter completely.

③ Beat the eggs on one plate and put the breadcrumbs on another. Dip the breasts in the egg, then the breadcrumbs, to coat completely, then repeat. Chill the chicken for at least 30 minutes.

④ Heat enough oil to cover the base of a large frying pan (skillet). When hot, turn the heat down fairly low. Fry (sauté) the chicken for about 6 minutes on each side until golden, crisp and cooked through.

⑤ Drain on kitchen paper (paper towels) and serve straight away with Sauté Potatoes and broccoli.

PREPARATION TIME: 20 MINUTES PLUS CHILLING
COOKING TIME: 12 MINUTES

Coq au Vin in a Pan

SERVES 4

30 ml/2 tbsp olive oil
1 onion, chopped
100 g/4 oz lardons
100 g/4 oz button mushrooms, sliced
4 skinless chicken breasts
Salt and freshly ground black pepper
300 ml/½ pt/1¼ cups red wine
150 ml/¼ pt/⅔ cup chicken stock, made with ½ stock cube
1 bouquet garni sachet
30 ml/2 tbsp plain (all-purpose) flour
30 ml/2 tbsp brandy
30 ml/2 tbsp chopped fresh parsley
To serve:
French bread and a green salad

① Heat the oil in a large frying pan (skillet)and fry (sauté) the onion and lardons, stirring, for 2 minutes.

② Stir in the mushrooms and cook, stirring, for 1 minute. Add the chicken and cook for 1 minute on each side to seal. Season with salt and pepper

③ Add the wine and stock to the pan with the bouquet garni. Bring to the boil, stirring gently. Reduce the heat, cover with a lid or foil and cook gently for 25 minutes or until the chicken is cooked through.

④ Remove the bouquet garni. Transfer the chicken breasts to a plate and keep warm in a low oven.

⑤ Blend the flour with the brandy. Stir into the frying pan and cook, stirring, for 2 minutes. Return the chicken to the pan and turn over in the sauce.

⑥ Transfer the chicken and sauce to warm plates. Garnish with the chopped parsley and serve with French bread and a green salad.

PREPARATION TIME: 6 MINUTES
COOKING TIME: 30–35 MINUTES

Fragrant Fried Poussins
SERVES 4

You can make this with other soft-leafed herbs – try basil or tarragon, for a change. The Hot Potato Salad on page 111 makes a delicious alternative accompaniment. Use chicken portions instead of halved poussins (Cornish hens) if you prefer.

2 large poussins
20 fresh sage leaves
1 small onion, grated
Salt and freshly ground black pepper
50 g/2 oz/¼ cup butter
30 ml/2 tbsp olive oil
Wedges of lemon
A few sprigs of fresh parsley
To serve:
Honeyed Corn Cobs (see page 116) and a crisp mixed salad

① Halve the poussins lengthways. Wipe both sides with kitchen paper (paper towels).

② Loosen the skin of each half and push in five sage leaves, spreading them out between the skin and flesh. Smear a little of the grated onion over the leaves. Season the skin with salt and pepper.

③ Heat the butter and oil in a large frying pan (skillet). Cook the poussin halves, skin-sides down, for 5 minutes until golden. Turn over, reduce the heat to moderate and continue to cook for 25 minutes or until cooked through and a rich golden brown.

④ Transfer to warm plates and spoon the buttery juices over. Garnish with wedges of lemon and sprigs of parsley and serve with Honeyed Corn Cobs and a crisp mixed salad.

PREPARATION TIME: 10 MINUTES
COOKING TIME: 30 MINUTES

Duck Breasts with Raspberries on Wilted Spinach

SERVES 4

4 small duck breasts, with skin
1.5 ml/¼ tsp salt
2.5 ml/½ tsp ground mace
30 ml/2 tbsp olive oil
150 ml/¼ pt/⅔ cup Chardonnay or other well-flavoured white wine
150 ml/¼ pt/⅔ cup chicken stock, made with ½ stock cube
30 ml/2 tbsp redcurrant jelly (clear conserve)
10 ml/2 tsp tomato purée (paste)
Freshly ground black pepper
450 g/1 lb baby spinach leaves
100 g/4 oz fresh raspberries
To serve:
New potatoes

① From the underside of the duck breasts, carefully cut off the sinew that runs from the pointed end, to stop them curling up when cooked. Turn over and score the skin in a criss-cross pattern with a sharp knife, then rub the skin with the salt mixed with the mace.

② Heat the oil in a large frying pan (skillet). Add the duck breasts, skin-sides down, and fry (sauté) for 5 minutes until a rich golden brown. Turn over and cook for a further 5 minutes until the duck is tender and still slightly pink in the centre. If you like duck well done, cook for a minute or two longer. Remove from the pan and keep warm in a low oven.

③ Stir the wine, stock, redcurrant jelly and tomato purée into the pan juices. Cook, stirring, until bubbling and smooth. Season to taste.

④ Meanwhile, wash the spinach well. Place in a large bowl. Pour boiling water over and leave to stand for 3 minutes. Drain thoroughly in a colander.

⑤ Add the raspberries to the sauce.

⑥ Pile the spinach on four warm plates. Slice the duck breasts diagonally with a sharp knife and arrange the slices over the spinach. Spoon the sauce over and serve with new potatoes.

PREPARATION TIME: 10 MINUTES
COOKING TIME: 12–15 MINUTES

Pork and Water Chestnut Stir-fry
SERVES 4

1 onion, halved and cut into chunky pieces
15 ml/1 tbsp sunflower oil
350 g/12 oz pork stir-fry meat
2 heads of pak choi, shredded
1 garlic clove, finely chopped
225 g/8 oz/1 small can of water chestnuts, drained and sliced
1.5 ml/¼ tsp Chinese five-spice powder
30 ml/2 tbsp soy sauce
To serve:
Egg Fried Rice (see page 123)

① Separate the onion pieces into layers.

② Heat the oil in a large frying pan (skillet). Add the onion and stir-fry for 2 minutes. Add the pork and stir-fry for 3 minutes.

③ Add the pak choi, garlic, water chestnuts and five-spice powder. Stir-fry for a further 2–3 minutes until cooked to your liking. Stir in the soy sauce and serve hot with Egg Fried Rice.

PREPARATION TIME: 5 MINUTES
COOKING TIME: 7–8 MINUTES

Gingered Duck Fans
SERVES 4

4 duck breasts
2.5 cm/1 in piece of fresh root ginger, peeled
Salt and freshly ground black pepper
20 g/¾ oz/1½ tbsp butter or margarine
150 ml/¼ pt/⅔ cup chicken stock, made with ½ stock cube
60 ml/4 tbsp ginger wine
10 ml/2 tsp cornflour (cornstarch)
15 ml/1 tbsp soy sauce
15 ml/1 tbsp water
A few sprigs of fresh parsley
Wedges of lime
To serve:
Crispy Noodle Cake (see page 121) and a beansprout salad

① From the underside of the duck breasts, remove the sinew that runs from the pointed end, to stop them curling up when cooked.

② Cut the ginger in half and rub the duck all over with the cut sides. Discard the ginger. Season the duck with salt and pepper.

③ Heat the butter or margarine in a large frying pan (skillet). Add the duck breasts, skin-sides down, and cook for about 5 minutes until golden. Turn over and cook the other sides for about 5 more minutes or until slightly pink in the centre. Cook a little longer if you like your duck well done. Remove from the pan and keep warm.

④ Add the stock and ginger wine to the pan and bring to the boil.

⑤ Blend the cornflour with the soy sauce and water and stir in. Bring back to the boil and cook for 1 minute until slightly thickened, stirring all the time. Season to taste.

⑥ With a sharp knife, slice the breasts lengthways and fan out on warm plates. Pour any juices back into the sauce.

⑦ Spoon the sauce around the breasts and garnish with sprigs of parsley and wedges of lime. Serve with Crispy Noodle Cake and a beansprout salad.

PREPARATION TIME: 10 MINUTES
COOKING TIME: 12–15 MINUTES

Melting Turkey Rolls
SERVES 4

4 turkey breast steaks
Salt and freshly ground black pepper
30 ml/2 tbsp tomato purée (paste)
30 ml/2 tbsp stoned (pitted) black olives, finely chopped
12 fresh basil leaves
4 slices of Cheddar or Gruyère (Swiss) cheese
4 slices of Parma ham
30 ml/2 tbsp olive oil
To serve:
Buttered noodles and a crisp green salad

① Put the turkey steaks, one at a time, between sheets of clingfilm (plastic wrap) and beat with a rolling pin or meat mallet to flatten.

② Remove from the clingfilm and season with salt and pepper, then spread with the tomato purée. Sprinkle the olives over, then lay three basil leaves and a slice of cheese on top of each one. Roll up, then roll each in a slice of Parma ham.

③ Heat the oil in a frying pan (skillet). Add the rolls and cook over a fairly low heat for 15 minutes, turning a little every few minutes until cooked through and golden all over.

④ Transfer to warm plates. Spoon over the pan juices, if liked, and serve hot with buttered noodles and a crisp green salad.

PREPARATION TIME: 10 MINUTES
COOKING TIME: 15 MINUTES

Chicken Chow

SERVES 4

125 g/4½ oz/½ packet of Chinese egg noodles
15 ml/1 tbsp sunflower oil
1 bunch of spring onions (scallions), trimmed and cut
diagonally into short lengths
1 garlic clove, finely chopped
1 green (bell) pepper, cut into thin strips
350 g/12 oz chicken stir-fry meat
100 g/4 oz oyster mushrooms, sliced
10 ml/2 tsp sesame oil
50 g/2 oz/½ cup raw cashew nuts
15 ml/1 tbsp oyster sauce
15 ml/1 tbsp soy sauce
120 ml/4 fl oz/½ cup water

① Put the noodles in a bowl and cover with boiling water. Leave to stand, stirring once or twice, while you cook the rest of the dish.

② Heat the sunflower oil in a large frying pan (skillet). Add the spring onions, garlic, pepper, chicken and mushrooms and stir-fry for 4 minutes until the chicken is cooked.

③ Add the sesame oil, cashew nuts, the sauces and water. Stir-fry for a further 30 seconds.

④ Drain the noodles and add to the pan. Toss until everything is well mixed. Pile on warm plates or in shallow bowls and serve.

PREPARATION TIME: 8 MINUTES
COOKING TIME: 5–6 MINUTES

Turkey and Winter Vegetables in Ale

SERVES 4

This can also be made with chicken or diced pork leg.

15 g/½ oz/1 tbsp butter or margarine
1 large carrot, cut into small dice
½ small swede (rutabaga), cut into small dice
1 leek, sliced
2 potatoes, cut into small dice
350 g/12 oz diced turkey meat
30 ml/2 tbsp cornflour (cornstarch)
450 ml/¾ pt/2 cups beef stock, made with 1 stock cube
300 ml/½ pt/1¼ cups brown ale
2.5 ml/½ tsp dried mixed herbs
Salt and freshly ground black pepper
100 g/4 oz frozen peas
To serve:
Crusty bread

① Heat half the butter or margarine in a large frying pan (skillet). Add the prepared vegetables and fry (sauté), stirring, for 2 minutes. Remove from the pan with a draining spoon.

② Toss the turkey in the cornflour. Heat the remaining butter or margarine in the pan. Add the turkey and fry for 2 minutes, stirring.

③ Stir in the stock and ale and bring to the boil, stirring. Add the herbs and salt and pepper to taste. Reduce the heat, cover with a lid or foil and cook gently for 15 minutes. Add the peas and cook for a further 5 minutes. Taste and re-season if necessary.

④ Spoon into warm bowls and serve with lots of crusty bread.

PREPARATION TIME: 15 MINUTES
COOKING TIME: 25 MINUTES

Braised Pork in White Wine and Cream
SERVES 4

15 ml/1 tbsp sunflower oil
4 pork shoulder steaks
1 leek, sliced
1 onion, sliced
15 ml/1 tbsp plain (all-purpose) flour
300 ml/½ pt/1¼ cups medium-dry white wine
1.5 ml/¼ tsp dried oregano
Salt and freshly ground black pepper
100 g/4 oz button mushrooms, sliced
45 ml/3 tbsp single (light) cream
15 ml/1 tbsp chopped fresh parsley
To serve:
Rosti (see page 110) and a green salad

① Heat the oil in a large frying pan (skillet). Add the steaks and brown quickly on both sides.

② Remove from the pan and add the leek and onion. Fry (sauté) for 2 minutes, stirring. Stir in the flour and cook for 1 minute, stirring.

③ Remove from the heat and blend in the wine. Return to the heat and bring to the boil, stirring. Return the chops to the pan and season with the oregano, salt and pepper. Add the mushrooms.

④ Cover with a lid or foil, reduce the heat to low and cook gently for 1 hour or until the chops are really tender.

⑤ Transfer the meat to warm plates. Stir the cream into the sauce and reheat but do not allow to boil. Taste and re-season if necessary.

⑥ Spoon the sauce over the chops and sprinkle with the parsley. Serve with Rosti and a green salad.

PREPARATION TIME: 5 MINUTES
COOKING TIME: 1 HOUR 5 MINUTES

Pork and Rice Rissoles with Sage and Apple Salsa

SERVES 4

2 green eating (dessert) apples
5 ml/1 tsp lemon juice
6 chopped fresh sage leaves
3 spring onions (scallions), finely chopped
75 ml/5 tbsp crème fraîche
Salt and freshly ground black pepper
100 g/4 oz/1 cup cooked long-grain rice
350 g/12 oz minced (ground) pork
8 juniper berries, crushed
1 egg, beaten
15 ml/1 tbsp sunflower oil
To serve:
New potatoes and Sautéed Savoy with Pine Nuts (see
    page 112)

① Grate the apple, including the skin, discarding any that doesn't grate. Mix the grated apple with the lemon juice immediately to prevent browning. Stir in the sage, one-third of the chopped spring onions, the crème fraîche and seasoning to taste. Chill in the fridge while you make the rissoles.

② Mix the rice with the pork, the remaining spring onions, the juniper berries and some salt and pepper. Stir in the beaten egg to bind. Shape into eight small cakes.

③ Heat the oil in a large frying pan (skillet). Fry (sauté) the rissoles for about 4 minutes on each side until golden and cooked through. Drain on kitchen paper (paper towels).

④ Place on plates with the salsa spooned to one side and serve with new potatoes and Sautéed Savoy with Pine Nuts.

PREPARATION TIME: 15 MINUTES
COOKING TIME: 8 MINUTES

Pork Chops with Caramelised Pineapple

SERVES 4

1 fresh pineapple
4 pork chops
10 ml/2 tsp onion powder
Salt and freshly ground black pepper
30 ml/2 tbsp olive oil
25 g/1 oz/2 tbsp butter
30 ml/2 tbsp light brown sugar
1.5 ml/¼ tsp chilli powder
300 ml/½ pt/1¼ cups passata (sieved tomatoes)
Grated rind and juice of 1 small lemon
A few sprigs of fresh parsley
To serve:
Golden Scallops (see page 106) and broccoli

① Cut the green top and the base off the pineapple, then cut off all the skin. Cut the fruit into eight slices and remove the hard core from the centre of each slice.

② Sprinkle the chops with the onion powder and some salt and pepper.

③ Heat the oil in a frying pan (skillet). Add the chops and fry (sauté) for 5 minutes on each side until tender and cooked through. Transfer to a plate and keep warm in a low oven.

④ Melt the butter in the frying pan. Add the pineapple, sugar and chilli powder. Cook for 2 minutes, turn over and cook for a further 2–3 minutes until golden and caramelised. Remove from the pan and keep warm.

⑤ Add the passata, lemon rind and juice to the pan and bring to the boil, scraping up any sediment and stirring until it dissolves. Taste and re-season if necessary.

⑥ Spoon the sauce on to plates. Top with the pork chops, then the pineapple slices. Garnish with sprigs of parsley and serve with Golden Scallops and broccoli.

PREPARATION TIME: 8 MINUTES
COOKING TIME: ABOUT 20 MINUTES

Escalopes with Prunes and Feta Cheese
SERVES 4

4 veal, pork or turkey escalopes
100 g/4 oz/⅔ cup ready-to-eat dried prunes
100 g/4 oz Feta cheese
2.5 ml/½ tsp dried oregano
1 egg, beaten
50 g/2 oz/1 cup fresh white breadcrumbs
Sunflower oil, for shallow-frying
Wedges of lemon
A handful of black olives
A few sprigs of fresh coriander (cilantro)
To serve:
Sauté Potatoes (see page 107) and a tomato and green
  (bell) pepper salad

① Put the escalopes between two sheets of clingfilm (plastic wrap) and beat with a rolling pin or meat mallet until very thin.

② Remove the clingfilm and cut the escalopes in half. Top four of the halves with the prunes.

③ Cut the cheese into thin slices (don't worry if it crumbles). Arrange over the prunes and sprinkle with the oregano. Top with the other halves of the escalopes and press together firmly.

④ Dip in the beaten egg, then the breadcrumbs, to coat completely.

⑤ Heat enough oil to coat the base of a large frying pan (skillet). Add the escalopes and fry (sauté) gently for about 8 minutes on each side until browned and cooked through. Drain on kitchen paper (paper towels).

⑥ Transfer to warm plates, garnish with wedges of lemon, black olives and coriander sprigs and serve with Sauté Potatoes and a tomato and green pepper salad.

PREPARATION TIME: 20 MINUTES
COOKING TIME: 15–20 MINUTES

Venison Steaks with Port and Cranberry Sauce

SERVES 4

This is also good with beef or lamb steaks. If you can get fresh cranberries, add a few to the pan with the marinade to give a lovely, sharp contrast to the rich sauce.

4 venison steaks, about 150 g/5 oz each
60 ml/4 tbsp olive oil
90 ml/6 tbsp port
60 ml/4 tbsp cranberry juice
15 ml/1 tbsp lemon juice
Salt and freshly ground black pepper
A sprig of fresh rosemary
15 g/½ oz/1 tbsp butter
45 ml/3 tbsp cranberry sauce
10 ml/2 tsp tomato purée (paste)
30 ml/2 tbsp chopped fresh parsley
A few sprigs of fresh parsley
To serve:
Creamed potatoes and a watercress and orange salad

① Wipe the steaks and place in a shallow dish.

② Whisk the oil, port and cranberry and lemon juices with a little salt and pepper and pour over. Add the sprig of rosemary. Cover and leave to marinate for 3 hours.

③ Heat the butter in a large frying pan (skillet). Lift the steaks out of the marinade, discarding the rosemary.

④ Add the steaks to the pan and brown quickly on both sides. Turn down the heat and cook for a further 3 minutes on each side until just cooked through. Transfer to a plate and keep warm in a low oven.

⑤ Add the marinade and cranberry sauce to the pan with the tomato purée and chopped parsley. Bring to the boil, stirring. Taste and re-season if necessary.

⑥ Transfer the steaks to warm serving plates. Pour any juices back into the sauce, stir then spoon over the venison. Garnish with sprigs of parsley and serve with creamed potatoes and a watercress and orange salad.

PREPARATION TIME: 5 MINUTES PLUS MARINATING
COOKING TIME: 8–10 MINUTES

Vegetarian Dishes

*V*egetables are delicious just tossed quickly in a pan, and all these dishes are truly mouth-watering and quick to make. They are also highly nutritious, with a balance of protein and carbohydrates and plenty of vitamins and minerals too. Most are low in fat, but, again, there are exceptions, like the Cheese and Celery Pasties – crisp, puffy, pan-fried pies that melt in the mouth and are simply irresistible.

Savoury-stuffed Gem Squash
SERVES 4

Substitute four thick slices of marrow (squash) for the whole little gem squash, if you prefer. Any leftover stock can be used for soup.

4 whole little gem squash
25 g/1 oz/2 tbsp long-grain rice
425 g/15 oz/1 large can of ratatouille
100 g/4 oz minced (ground) Quorn
30 ml/2 tbsp chopped fresh basil
Salt and freshly ground black pepper
25 g/1 oz/¼ cup pine nuts, toasted
600 ml/1 pt/2½ cups vegetable stock, made with 2 stock
  cubes
To serve:
Freshly grated Parmesan cheese, crusty bread and
  a green salad

① Cut the tops off the squash and scoop out the seeds and pith with a spoon. Stand the squash up in a large frying pan (skillet).

② Mix the rice with the ratatouille, quorn, basil and some salt and pepper. Spoon the filling into each squash, packing it down well. Scatter the pine nuts over the top.

③ Pour the stock around.

④ Bring to the boil, reduce the heat, cover with a lid or foil and cook gently for 30 minutes until the squash and rice are tender.

⑤ Transfer to warm plates and serve with grated Parmesan cheese, crusty bread and a green salad.

PREPARATION TIME: 8 MINUTES
COOKING TIME: 30 MINUTES

Sweetcorn and Banana Fritters with Satay Sauce

SERVES 4

2 spring onions (scallions), finely chopped
225 g/8 oz/1 cup smooth peanut butter
15 ml/1 tbsp light brown sugar
15 ml/1 tbsp soy sauce
A few drops of Tabasco sauce
100 g/4 oz/1 cup plain (all-purpose) flour
1.5 ml/¼ tsp salt
1 egg, separated
200 g/7 oz/1 small can of sweetcorn (corn)
4 bananas
Groundnut (peanut) or corn oil, for deep-frying
Wedges of lime
A few sprigs of fresh parsley
To serve:
A large mixed salad

① Put the spring onions and 100 ml/3½ fl oz/scant ½ cup water in a small saucepan. Bring to the boil and cook for 2 minutes.

② Add the peanut butter, sugar, soy sauce and Tabasco to taste, and stir until thick and smooth. Remove from the heat.

③ Put the flour in a bowl with the salt. Make a well in the centre and add the egg yolk. Gradually mix in 150 ml/ ¼ pt/⅔ cup water to form a smooth, thick batter.

④ Whisk the egg white until stiff and fold in with a metal spoon.

⑤ Drain the sweetcorn well and dry on kitchen paper (paper towels). Peel the bananas and cut each one into four chunks.

⑥ Pour about 2 cm/¾ in oil into a large frying pan (skillet) and heat until a cube of day-old bread browns in 30 seconds. Dip the banana chunks in the batter and fry (sauté) for about 3 minutes until golden brown, turning once. Remove with a draining spoon, drain on kitchen paper and keep warm in a low oven.

⑦ Add the sweetcorn to the remaining batter. Reheat the oil, drop spoonfuls of the corn batter into the oil and fry for about 3 minutes until golden, turning once. Remove with a draining spoon and drain on kitchen paper.

⑧ Meanwhile, reheat the sauce and add a little more water if necessary, to make a thick, dipping sauce. Spoon into small pots.

⑨ Pile the sweetcorn and banana fritters on warm plates and put a pot of sauce to one side. Garnish with wedges of lime and sprigs of parsley and serve with a large mixed salad.

PREPARATION TIME: 10 MINUTES
COOKING TIME: 6–8 MINUTES

Smoked Tofu Croquettes with Hoisin Dressing

SERVES 4

1 large potato
225 g/8 oz/1 cup smoked tofu, drained and chopped
1 small onion, grated
30 ml/2 tbsp chopped fresh coriander (cilantro) or parsley
1.5 ml/¼ tsp ground ginger
Salt and freshly ground black pepper
1 egg, separated
50 g/2 oz/½ cup dried breadcrumbs
30 ml/2 tbsp hoisin sauce
15 ml/1 tbsp soy sauce
30 ml/2 tbsp dry sherry
15 ml/1 tbsp sunflower oil, plus extra for cooking
15 ml/1 tbsp tomato ketchup (catsup)
15 ml/1 tbsp clear honey
30 ml/2 tbsp pure orange juice
100 g/4 oz/2 cups beansprouts
¼ head of Chinese leaves (stem lettuce), shredded
1 carrot, cut into ribbons with a potato peeler
¼ cucumber, cut into ribbons with a potato peeler

① Boil the potato in water until tender, then drain. Alternatively, prick all over and cook in the microwave for about 4 minutes. When cool enough to handle, peel off the skin and place in a large bowl. Mash with a fork.

② Add the tofu, onion, coriander or parsley, ginger, salt and pepper and mix with egg yolk to bind. Shape into eight croquettes.

③ Lightly beat the egg white and brush all over the croquettes, then roll in the breadcrumbs to coat completely. Chill until ready to cook.

④ Mix together the hoisin sauce, soy sauce, sherry, oil, ketchup, honey and orange juice and reserve.

⑤ Mix the beansprouts with the Chinese leaves, carrot and cucumber and pile on plates.

⑥ Heat enough oil to cover the base of a large frying pan (skillet) and fry (sauté) the croquettes for about 6 minutes, turning frequently, until golden all round and cooked through.

⑦ Drain on kitchen paper (paper towels). Trickle the dressing over the salads, then put two croquettes on top of each pile. Serve straight away.

PREPARATION TIME: 15–25 MINUTES
(DEPENDING ON COOKING TIME OF POTATO)
COOKING TIME: 6 MINUTES

Cheese and Celery Pasties

SERVES 4

These are not for the calorie-conscious but they are so delicious, they are worth breaking any diet for! If you don't have a very large frying pan (skillet), cook the pies in two batches, keeping one batch warm in a low oven.

100 g/4 oz/1 cup Cheddar cheese, grated
1 celery stick, finely sliced
1 potato, grated
1 carrot, grated
2 spring onions (scallions), finely chopped
Salt and freshly ground black pepper
350 g/12 oz puff pastry (paste)
Groundnut (peanut) or corn oil, for deep-frying
To serve:
Pickles and a tomato salad

① Mix the cheese, celery, potato, carrot and spring onions in a bowl with a little salt and lots of pepper.

② Cut the pastry into quarters and roll each thinly to an oblong about 20 × 10 cm/8 × 4 in (they don't need to be too exact).

③ Pile cheese mixture in the centre of each piece of pastry. Brush the edges with water.

④ Fold the pastry up over the filling, pressing the edges together, then roll them over all round to seal and form a pasty shape.

⑤ Pour about 2 cm/¾ in oil into a large frying pan and heat until a cube of day-old bread browns in 40 seconds. Add the pies and cook for about 6 minutes, turning once or twice, until puffy, golden and the filling is cooked through. Drain on kitchen paper (paper towels).

⑥ Serve with pickles and a tomato salad.

PREPARATION TIME: 20 MINUTES
COOKING TIME: 6 MINUTES

Chickpeas and Spinach in Creamy Paprika Sauce

SERVES 4

450 g/1 lb spinach
Salt and freshly ground black pepper
15 ml/1 tbsp sunflower oil
1 onion, chopped
15 ml/1 tbsp paprika
400 g/14 oz/1 large can of chopped tomatoes
15 ml/1 tbsp tomato purée (paste)
90 ml/6 tbsp crème fraîche
5 ml/1 tsp caster (superfine) sugar
2 x 425 g/15 oz/large cans of chickpeas (garbanzos), drained
15 ml/1 tbsp chopped fresh parsley
To serve:
Pan Garlic Bread (see page 139)

① Wash the spinach well and shake off the excess water. Tear into pieces, discarding any thick stalks. Place in a large frying pan (skillet) and sprinkle lightly with salt and pepper.

② Cook over a moderate heat, stirring frequently, for 4–5 minutes until tender and wilted. Drain in a colander, pressing out all the excess moisture and reserve.

③ Wipe out the frying pan with kitchen paper (paper towels) if necessary, then heat the oil. Fry (sauté) the onion gently for 3 minutes, stirring until softened but not browned.

④ Add the paprika, tomatoes and tomato purée and cook, stirring, for 5 minutes until pulpy. Stir in 60 ml/4 tbsp of the crème fraîche, the sugar, spinach and drained chickpeas. Heat through, stirring. Taste and re-season if necessary.

⑤ Spoon the mixture into warm bowls. Add a spoonful of the remaining crème fraîche and a sprinkling of parsley to each and serve hot with Pan Garlic Bread.

PREPARATION TIME: 10 MINUTES
COOKING TIME: 15 MINUTES

Cracked Wheat with Puy Lentil Braise
SERVES 4

225 g/8 oz/2 cups bulghar (cracked wheat)
1 garlic clove, crushed (optional)
600 ml/1 pt/2½ cups boiling water
45 ml/3 tbsp olive oil
1 onion, chopped
1 green (bell) pepper, diced
175 g/6 oz/1 cup puy lentils
450 ml/¾ pt/2 cups vegetable stock, made with 1 stock
   cube
225 g/8 oz/1 small can of chopped tomatoes
10 ml/2 tsp tomato purée (paste)
1.5 ml/¼ tsp ground cinnamon
1.5 ml/¼ tsp ground cumin
Salt and freshly ground black pepper
50 g/2 oz/⅓ cup raisins
50 g/2 oz/½ cup toasted flaked (slivered) almonds
30 ml/2 tbsp chopped fresh parsley
30 ml/2 tbsp chopped fresh mint
15 ml/1 tbsp lemon juice
To serve:
A crisp green salad

① Put the bulghar in a bowl. Add the garlic, if using, and water and stir. Place the bowl over a pan of gently simmering water. Cover with a lid or foil and leave for 30 minutes.

② Meanwhile, heat 15 ml/1 tbsp of the oil in a frying pan (skillet). Add the onion and pepper and fry (sauté) for 3 minutes until turning slightly golden.

③ Add the lentils, stock, tomatoes, tomato purée, cinnamon, cumin and some salt and pepper. Bring to the boil, stirring, reduce the heat to moderate and simmer for about 20 minutes until nearly all the liquid has evaporated and the lentils are just tender but still have some 'bite'.

④ Stir the raisins, almonds, herbs, lemon juice and remaining oil into the bulghar. Season to taste with salt and pepper.

⑤ Spoon the bulghar on to warm plates and spoon the lentil braise to one side. Serve straight away with a crisp green salad.

PREPARATION TIME: 10 MINUTES
COOKING TIME: 30 MINUTES

Quorn Provençal
SERVES 4

15 ml/1 tbsp olive oil
1 red onion, finely chopped
1 garlic clove, crushed
1 green (bell) pepper, chopped
400 g/14 oz/1 large can of chopped tomatoes
15 ml/1 tbsp tomato purée (paste)
2 sun-dried tomatoes, drained and chopped
75 ml/5 tbsp dry white wine
2.5 ml/½ tsp herbes de Provence
30 ml/2 tbsp sliced black olives
5 ml/1 tsp caster (superfine) sugar
Salt and freshly ground black pepper
225 g/8 oz Quorn pieces
15 ml/1 tbsp chopped fresh parsley
To serve:
Plain rice and a green salad

① Heat the oil in a large frying pan (skillet) and fry (sauté) the onion, garlic and pepper, stirring, for 3 minutes.

② Add the canned tomatoes, tomato purée, sun-dried tomatoes and wine. Bring to the boil, add the herbs, olives, sugar and seasoning and simmer gently for 5 minutes.

③ Add the Quorn pieces and cook, stirring occasionally, for a further 5 minutes. Taste and re-season if necessary.

④ Spoon on to a bed of rice, garnish with chopped parsley and serve with a green salad.

PREPARATION TIME: 8 MINUTES
COOKING TIME: 12–15 MINUTES

Oriental Vegetable Stir-fry

SERVES 4

100 g/4 oz cellophane (rice) noodles
10 ml/2 tsp sunflower oil
5 ml/1 tsp sesame oil
1 bunch of spring onions (scallions), cut diagonally into
  short lengths
1 red (bell) pepper, cut into thin strips
1 green pepper, cut into thin strips
225 g/8 oz/1 small can of bamboo shoots, drained
1 carrot, cut into thin matchsticks
5 cm/2 in piece of cucumber, cut into thin matchsticks
100 g/4 oz/2 cups beansprouts
225 g/8 oz/1 small can of pineapple pieces in natural juice
10 ml/2 tsp cornflour (cornstarch)
15 ml/1 tbsp tomato purée (paste)
30 ml/2 tbsp soy sauce
15 ml/1 tbsp red wine vinegar
10 ml/2 tsp light brown sugar
50 g/2 oz/½ cup raw cashew nuts

① Soak the noodles in boiling water while cooking the stir-fry.

② Heat the oils in a large frying pan (skillet). Add all the prepared vegetables except the cucumber and beansprouts and stir-fry for 4 minutes.

③ Add the cucumber and beansprouts and stir for 1 minute.

④ Blend a little of the pineapple juice with the cornflour in a cup. Add the remaining juice and pineapple to the vegetables with the tomato purée, soy sauce, vinegar and sugar. Stir in the blended cornflour and bring to the boil, stirring until slightly thickened.

⑤ Drain the noodles and pile on warm plates. Spoon the stir-fry over and sprinkle with the cashew nuts.

PREPARATION TIME: 20 MINUTES
COOKING TIME: 6–7 MINUTES

Tuscan Broccoli and Beans

SERVES 4

450 g/1 lb broccoli, cut into small florets
15 ml/1 tbsp olive oil
1 onion, roughly chopped
1 garlic clove, crushed
1 red (bell) pepper, diced
400 g/14 oz/1 large can of chopped tomatoes
425 g/15 oz/1 large can of haricot (navy) beans, drained
2.5 ml/½ tsp dried oregano
2 sun-dried tomatoes, chopped
Salt and freshly ground black pepper
50 g/2 oz/½ cup Mozzarella cheese, grated
30 ml/2 tbsp sliced green olives
30 ml/2 tbsp chopped fresh basil
To serve:
Focaccia bread

① Put the broccoli in a large frying pan (skillet) and cover with lightly salted boiling water. Bring back to the boil, cover with a lid or foil and cook for 4–5 minutes until tender. Drain in a colander and keep warm in individual bowls in a low oven.

② Wipe out the pan with kitchen paper (paper towels) if necessary, then heat the oil and fry (sauté) the onion, garlic and pepper for 3 minutes, stirring.

③ Add the canned tomatoes and beans, the oregano, sun-dried tomatoes and some salt and pepper. Bring back to the boil, reduce the heat and simmer for 5 minutes. Taste and re-season if necessary.

④ Spoon over the broccoli, sprinkle with the Mozzarella, olives and basil and serve straight away with focaccia bread.

PREPARATION TIME: 15 MINUTES
COOKING TIME: 12–15 MINUTES

Vegetable Curry Cake
SERVES 4

1 large potato
1 large sweet potato
1 large carrot
1 onion
15 ml/1 tbsp garam masala
1.5 ml/¼ tsp chilli powder
Salt and freshly ground black pepper
15 ml/1 tbsp sunflower oil
225 g/8 oz/1 small can of pease pudding
15 ml/1 tbsp curry paste
15 ml/1 tbsp smooth mango chutney
300 ml/½ pt/1¼ cups vegetable stock, made with 1 stock
  cube
50 g/2 oz creamed coconut
30 ml/2 tbsp chopped fresh coriander (cilantro)
Lettuce leaves
Slices of tomato and cucumber
Wedges of lemon

① Scrub the potato and peel the sweet potato, carrot and onion. Grate all the vegetables into a bowl. Squeeze the mixture thoroughly and drain off the excess moisture. Stir in the spices and season well.

② Heat the oil in a large frying pan (skillet). Add the grated vegetable mixture and press down well. Cover and cook over a gentle heat for 15 minutes. Remove the lid, turn up the heat to moderate and cook for a further 15 minutes until the cake is tender and the base golden brown. Turn out on to a warm plate, browned side up, and keep warm in a low oven.

③ Empty the pease pudding into the pan and stir in the curry paste, mango chutney, stock and coconut. Cook, stirring, until blended and bubbling. Season to taste and add half the coriander.

④ Cut the cake into wedges and transfer to warm plates. Spoon the sauce over, sprinkle with the remaining coriander and garnish with the salad stuffs and wedges of lemon.

PREPARATION TIME: 15 MINUTES
COOKING TIME: 35 MINUTES

Mexican Eggs
SERVES 4

30 ml/2 tbsp olive oil
1 large onion, chopped
1 aubergine (eggplant), diced
1 green (bell) pepper, diced
1 red chilli, seeded and chopped
425 g/15 oz/1 large can of black-eye beans, drained
30 ml/2 tbsp tomato relish
150 ml/¼ pt/⅔ cup water or vegetable stock, made with
  ½ stock cube
Salt and freshly ground black pepper
4 eggs
To serve:
Tortilla chips and a green salad

① Heat the oil in a large frying pan (skillet). Add the onion, aubergine, pepper and chilli and fry (sauté), stirring, for 5 minutes until softened.

② Add the beans, relish, water or stock and some salt and pepper and stir well. Cover and simmer gently for 10 minutes until the vegetables are tender and nearly all the liquid has evaporated.

③ Make four wells in the mixture and break an egg into each. Cover with a lid or foil and cook for 5–10 minutes until cooked to your liking.

④ Serve straight from the pan with tortilla chips and a salad.

PREPARATION TIME: 10 MINUTES
COOKING TIME: 20–25 MINUTES

Mixed Mushroom Risotto

SERVES 4

Variety packs of mushrooms, containing oyster, chestnut, chanterelles, etc., are ideal for this. Use a potato peeler to shave the Parmesan cheese.

15 ml/1 tbsp olive oil
2 onions, chopped
1 garlic clove, crushed
225 g/8 oz mixed mushrooms, sliced
225 g/8 oz/1 cup risotto rice
750 ml/1¼ pts/3 cups hot vegetable stock, made with
   2 stock cubes
2.5 ml/½ tsp dried oregano
Salt and freshly ground black pepper
30 ml/2 tbsp chopped fresh parsley
25 g/1 oz/¼ cup shavings of Parmesan cheese
To serve:
Focaccia bread and an avocado and tomato salad

① Heat the oil in a large frying pan (skillet). Add the onions, garlic and mushrooms and cook gently, stirring, for 2 minutes until softened but not browned.

② Add the rice and stir until every grain of rice is glistening.

③ Pour in a quarter of the stock and add the oregano. Allow to simmer gently, stirring occasionally, until the liquid has been absorbed. Repeat, adding the stock a little at a time, until all the stock is used and the risotto is creamy but still has some 'bite'. It should take about 20 minutes in all. Season to taste.

④ Spoon the risotto on to warm plates. Sprinkle with parsley and scatter with the flakes of Parmesan. Serve hot with focaccia bread and an avocado and tomato salad.

PREPARATION TIME: 10 MINUTES
COOKING TIME: 25 MINUTES

Side Dishes and Accompaniments

Your frying pan (skillet) can cook up a multitude of delicious dishes to brighten up any meat, fish, poultry or vegetarian main course. Cooking quickly preserves nutrients, colour and flavour and all the recipes in this section are easy to prepare and fast to cook, which makes them ideal to serve as part of any meal.

Golden Scallops
SERVES 4

You can vary the quantity of potatoes, according to appetites.

4–6 potatoes
Iced water
Sunflower or corn oil, for shallow-frying
Salt

① Peel the potatoes and cut into slices 5 mm/¼ in thick. Drop into a bowl of iced water and leave to stand for 15 minutes.

② Heat about 5 mm/¼ in of oil in a large frying pan (skillet) until a cube of day-old bread browns in 30 seconds.

③ Drain the potatoes and dry thoroughly on kitchen paper (paper towels).

④ Hold a fish slice at the side of the frying pan and slide the potato slices down into the pan. Cook for 4–5 minutes, turning once or twice if necessary, until golden brown.

⑤ Remove from the pan with the fish slice and drain on kitchen paper. Sprinkle with salt and serve straight away.

PREPARATION TIME: 8 MINUTES PLUS STANDING
COOKING TIME: 4–5 MINUTES

Sauté Potatoes

SERVES 4

4–6 potatoes
40 g/1½ oz/3 tbsp butter or margarine
30 ml/2 tbsp sunflower or olive oil
Salt

① Peel the potatoes, cut into small dice and place in a pan of cold water. Bring to the boil and boil for 2 minutes.

② Drain the cubes and dry well on kitchen paper (paper towels).

③ Heat the butter or margarine and oil in a large frying pan (skillet). Add the potatoes and fry (sauté) for about 5 minutes, turning occasionally, until golden brown and cooked through.

④ Drain on kitchen paper, sprinkle with salt and serve hot.

PREPARATION TIME: 10 MINUTES
COOKING TIME: 5 MINUTES

Variations

Sauté potatoes with garlic: Add 1 or 2 halved garlic cloves to the pan whilst frying (sautéeing) the potatoes and discard before serving.

Sauté potatoes with sesame seeds: Sprinkle the cooked potatoes with 30 ml/2 tbsp sesame seeds before serving.

Sauté potatoes with spices: Combine a good pinch each of chilli and mixed (apple-pie) spice with a good pinch of celery salt and toss the cooked potatoes in this before serving.

Bobbed and Squashed

SERVES 4

This is a variation on traditional Bubble and Squeak!

30 ml/2 tbsp sunflower oil
1 large onion, chopped
5 ml/1 tsp ground cumin
350 g/12 oz cooked leftover potato
100 g/4 oz cooked leftover carrots
50 g/2 oz cooked leftover peas
Salt and freshly ground black pepper
15 ml/1 tbsp chopped fresh coriander (cilantro)

① Heat the oil in a large frying pan (skillet). Add the onion and cumin and fry (sauté) for 3 minutes, stirring, until softened and lightly golden.

② Meanwhile, chop the potato and carrots and mix with the peas. Add to the pan and stir well. Season liberally with salt, pepper and the coriander. Cook, pressing down well, for about 10 minutes until piping hot and crisp and golden underneath.

③ Turn out on to a warm plate and serve piping hot.

PREPARATION TIME: 5 MINUTES
COOKING TIME: 15 MINUTES

Pan Dauphinoise
SERVES 4

---

450 g/1 lb potatoes, thinly sliced
15 g/½ oz/1 tbsp butter
1 large garlic clove, crushed
100 g/4 oz/1 cup Gruyère (Swiss) cheese, grated
Salt and freshly ground black pepper
300 ml/½ pt/1¼ cups double (heavy) cream
1 egg

---

① Put the potatoes in a large frying pan (skillet). Cover with water, bring to the boil and cook for 4 minutes. Drain in a colander.

② Wipe out the pan with kitchen paper (paper towels). Spread the butter all over the base.

③ Layer the potatoes with tiny flecks of the garlic and cheese and season with salt and pepper.

④ Whisk the cream and egg together and pour over. Cook over a high heat until beginning to bubble round the edges, then turn down the heat, cover with a lid or foil and cook gently for 30 minutes until set.

⑤ If liked, flash under a hot grill (broiler) to brown. Serve straight from the pan.

PREPARATION TIME: 10 MINUTES
COOKING TIME: 30–35 MINUTES

Rosti

SERVES 4

You can make one big cake if you prefer. You can also vary the flavour by adding spices, a little chopped, fried (sautéed) bacon, some drained, canned sweetcorn (corn) or a little finely chopped (bell) pepper.

4 potatoes, grated
1 onion, grated
Salt and freshly ground black pepper
15 ml/1 tbsp sunflower oil

① Squeeze the grated potato to remove excess moisture. Mix with the onion and some salt and pepper. Divide the potato mixture into four flat cakes.

② Heat the oil in a large frying pan (skillet) and fry the cakes for about 5 minutes, pressing them down firmly with a fish slice. Turn over and cook the other sides for a further 5 minutes or until golden and cooked through.

③ Transfer to warm plates and serve hot.

PREPARATION TIME: 8 MINUTES
COOKING TIME: 10 MINUTES

Hot Potato Salad

SERVES 4

This is delicious served with any hot or cold meat or poultry –
try it with my Fragrant Fried Poussins (see page 77). It also
makes a great lunch dish with a green salad.

700 g/1½ lb baby new potatoes, scrubbed
6 rashers (slices) of streaky bacon, rinded and diced
90 ml/6 tbsp boiling water
90 ml/6 tbsp white wine vinegar
60 ml/4 tbsp crème fraîche
1 spring onion (scallion), finely chopped
Salt and freshly ground black pepper

① Put the potatoes in a frying pan (skillet) and cover with lightly salted boiling water. Bring back to the boil, cover with a lid or foil and cook for about 10 minutes or until tender. Drain and tip the potatoes into a bowl. Keep warm.

② Heat the pan to remove any moisture, then add the bacon and dry-fry until crisp and brown. Remove from the pan with a draining spoon.

③ Add the measured boiling water to the pan with the vinegar and boil for 1 minute. Stir in the crème fraîche, spring onion (reserving a little of the green top for garnish), the bacon and some salt and pepper. Stir, then spoon over the potatoes, toss and sprinkle with the reserved onion before serving.

PREPARATION TIME: 5 MINUTES
COOKING TIME: 15 MINUTES

Sautéed Savoy with Pine Nuts

SERVES 4

25 g/1 oz/¼ cup pine nuts
15 ml/1 tbsp sunflower oil
½ savoy cabbage, finely shredded
30 ml/2 tbsp water
Salt and freshly ground black pepper

① Heat a large frying pan (skillet). Add the pine nuts and toss over the heat until lightly golden. Tip out of the pan.

② Heat the oil in the pan. Add the savoy cabbage and cook, stirring, for 1 minute. Add the water and cook for about 3 minutes until the cabbage is just tender but still bright green and tinged with gold in places.

③ Add the pine nuts and some salt and pepper, toss again and serve.

PREPARATION TIME: 5 MINUTES
COOKING TIME: 6 MINUTES

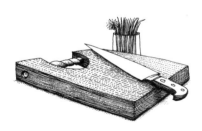

Parsnip and Walnut Cream

SERVES 4

3 parsnips, thinly sliced
Butter or margarine, for greasing
Salt and freshly ground black pepper
25 g/1 oz/¼ cup walnuts, finely chopped
300 ml/½ pt/1¼ cups double (heavy) cream
A little freshly grated nutmeg

① Put the parsnips in a large frying pan (skillet) and cover with boiling water. Boil for 3 minutes, then drain in a colander.

② Wipe out the pan and grease it with a little butter or margarine. Put a third of the parsnip slices back in the pan. Season and sprinkle with a third of the walnuts.

③ Repeat the layers until all the ingredients are used.

④ Pour over the cream and dust with a little grated nutmeg. Bring to the boil, turn down the heat to low, cover with a lid or foil and cook gently for 30 minutes until most of the cream has been absorbed into the parsnips and they are tender when pierced.

⑤ Serve straight from the pan.

PREPARATION TIME: 10 MINUTES
COOKING TIME: 30 MINUTES

Glazed Carrots

SERVES 4

2 large carrots, cut into matchsticks
150 ml/¼ pt/⅔ cup chicken or vegetable stock, made with
 ½ stock cube
15 ml/½ oz/1 tbsp butter or margarine
15 ml/1 tbsp light brown sugar
Salt and freshly ground black pepper
15 ml/1 tbsp chopped fresh parsley

① Put the carrots in a large frying pan (skillet) with the stock. Bring to the boil and cook for 3–4 minutes until almost tender and nearly all the stock has evaporated.

② Add the butter or margarine and sugar and season well. Cook, tossing gently, for about 2 minutes until glazed and just tender.

③ Sprinkle with the parsley and serve.

PREPARATION TIME: 5 MINUTES
COOKING TIME: 5–6 MINUTES

Creamy Mushrooms and Courgettes

SERVES 4

25 g/1 oz/2 tbsp butter or margarine
100 g/4 oz button mushrooms, quartered
3 small courgettes (zucchini), sliced
15 ml/1 tbsp water
2.5 ml/½ tsp dried thyme
Salt and freshly ground black pepper
45 ml/3 tbsp single (light) cream
15 ml/1 tbsp chopped fresh parsley

① Melt the butter or margarine in a large frying pan (skillet). Add the mushrooms and courgettes and toss for 1 minute.

② Add the water, thyme and some salt and pepper. Cover with a lid or foil and cook over a gentle heat, shaking the pan occasionally, for about 10 minutes or until the courgettes are just tender.

③ Stir in the cream and heat through but do not allow to boil. Sprinkle with the parsley and serve straight away.

PREPARATION TIME: 5 MINUTES
COOKING TIME: 12 MINUTES

Honeyed Corn Cobs

SERVES 4

3 corn cobs
A little salt
15 ml/1 tbsp clear honey
15 ml/½ oz/1 tbsp butter or margarine
Finely grated rind and juice of ½ lemon

① Cut each corn cob into four pieces with a large, sharp knife. Place in a large frying pan (skillet) and cover with boiling water. Add a good pinch of salt. Boil for 15–20 minutes until a kernel of corn pulls away easily. Drain off the water.

② Add the honey, butter or margarine and lemon rind and juice. Cook, tossing, for about 3 minutes until turning golden in places and stickily glazed.

③ Serve hot.

PREPARATION TIME: 5 MINUTES
COOKING TIME: 20–25 MINUTES

Re-fried beans
SERVES 4

Serve this spicy mixture in tacos, on tostadas (Mexican open sandwiches) or with any pan-fried meat or poultry. It also makes a great dip with tortilla chips.

15 ml/1 tbsp sunflower oil
425 g/15 oz/1 large can of pinto beans, drained
15 ml/1 tbsp chopped fresh parsley
5 ml/1 tsp dried oregano
A pinch of chilli powder
A pinch of ground cumin
Salt and freshly ground black pepper
50 g/2 oz/½ cup Cheddar cheese, grated

① Heat the oil in a frying pan (skillet).

② Mash the beans with a fork or purée them in a blender or food processor.

③ Add to the hot oil and sprinkle with all the remaining ingredients except the cheese. Cook, stirring, until piping hot.

④ Spoon on to plates and sprinkle with the cheese. Alternatively, stir the cheese into the mixture in the pan and heat until melted, then serve.

PREPARATION TIME: 3 MINUTES
COOKING TIME: 5 MINUTES

Garlic Mushrooms

SERVES 4

These are good with plain fried (sautéed) steaks, chops or chicken. They can also be served as a starter with crusty bread.

350 g/12 oz smallish, flat mushrooms
25 g/1 oz/2 tbsp butter or margarine
1 garlic clove, crushed
15 ml/1 tbsp chopped fresh parsley
Salt and freshly ground black pepper
75 ml/5 tbsp water

① Peel the mushrooms and trim the stalks.

② Melt the butter or margarine in a large frying pan (skillet). Add the mushrooms, peeled sides down, and cook for 2 minutes.

③ Sprinkle with the garlic, parsley and some salt and pepper. Pour in the water.

④ Bring to the boil, cover with a lid or foil and cook for 5 minutes. Remove the lid or foil and cook rapidly until the moisture is absorbed. Serve hot.

PREPARATION TIME: 8 MINUTES
COOKING TIME: 8–9 MINUTES

Mediterranean Vegetables

SERVES 4

If you are cooking for one, use half of one (bell) pepper rather than a quarter of two, if you prefer. However, it's best to cook at least enough for two people – the vegetable mixture is delicious cold as a salad the next day.

---

1 small red pepper, cut into 4 chunky slices
1 small green pepper, cut into 4 chunky slices
1 small aubergine (eggplant), sliced
1 courgette (zucchini), cut diagonally into slices
30 ml/2 tbsp olive oil
1 garlic clove, finely chopped
2 sun-dried tomatoes, finely chopped

---

① Toss the pepper, aubergine and courgette slices in the oil.

② Heat a large griddle or frying pan (skillet). Add the pepper slices and fry (sauté) for 2 minutes on each side. Push to one side of the pan.

③ Add the aubergine and fry for 1–2 minutes on each side. Repeat with the courgette slices.

④ Spread all the vegetables out again. Sprinkle with the garlic and sun-dried tomato. Turn down the heat and cook for a further 3 minutes, turning occasionally, until all the vegetables are just tender but still holding their shape. Serve hot.

PREPARATION TIME: 10 MINUTES
COOKING TIME: 10–15 MINUTES

Pan-roasted Vine Tomatoes

SERVES 4

---

30 ml/2 tbsp olive oil
4 sprigs of cherry tomatoes on the vine, each with
  4–5 tomatoes
5 ml/1 tsp caster (superfine) sugar
15 ml/1 tbsp balsamic vinegar
Salt and freshly ground black pepper

---

① Heat the oil in a large frying pan (skillet).

② Add the tomatoes and sprinkle with the sugar. Fry (sauté) for 2 minutes, then carefully turn the sprigs over.

③ Sprinkle with the balsamic vinegar and some salt and pepper. Cover and cook for a further 2–3 minutes until lightly coloured and almost tender but still holding their shape.

④ Transfer to warm plates, spoon any juices over and serve.

PREPARATION TIME: 2 MINUTES
COOKING TIME: 4–5 MINUTES

Crispy Noodle Cake

SERVES 4

You can make four individual cakes if you prefer –
it's easiest to cook them one or two at a time, so allow
more cooking time.

250 g/9 oz/1 medium packet of Chinese egg noodles
45 ml/3 tbsp sunflower oil

① Put the noodles in a large frying pan (skillet). Cover with boiling water. Bring back to the boil, then leave to stand for 5 minutes, breaking up the noodles after 2 minutes. Drain in a colander, then dry on kitchen paper (paper towels).

② Wipe out the pan with kitchen paper if necessary, then heat 30 ml/2 tbsp of the oil. Add the noodles and spread out. Fry (sauté) for about 4 minutes until golden underneath. Invert the cake on to a plate.

③ Heat the remaining oil in the pan. Slide the cake back into the pan and fry for a further 2–3 minutes until crisp and golden on the other side.

④ Serve the cake whole with any Asian-style dish spooned on top or cut into wedges to serve as an accompaniment.

PREPARATION TIME: 6 MINUTES
COOKING TIME: 6–7 MINUTES

Stir-fried Mangetout and Baby Sweetcorn

SERVES 4

---

15 ml/1 tbsp sunflower oil
100 g/4 oz baby sweetcorn cobs
2 spring onions (scallions), cut diagonally into slices
100 g/4 oz mangetout (snow peas)
5 ml/1 tsp soy sauce

---

① Heat the oil in a large frying pan (skillet). Add the baby corn cobs and spring onions and stir-fry for 2 minutes.

② Add the mangetout and continue to stir-fry for a further 2 minutes.

③ Sprinkle with the soy sauce, toss and serve.

PREPARATION TIME: 5 MINUTES
COOKING TIME: 4 MINUTES

Egg Fried Rice

SERVES 4

Turn this into Special Fried Rice by adding 50 g/2 oz cooked, peeled prawns (shrimp) and 50 g/2 oz finely diced cooked chicken to the rice before stirring in the egg.

30 ml/2 tbsp sunflower oil
350 g/12 oz/3 cups cooked long-grain rice
50 g/2 oz cooked peas
1 egg, beaten
A pinch of Chinese five-spice powder
5 ml/1 tsp soy sauce

① Heat the oil in a large frying pan (skillet). Add the rice and peas and toss, stirring, for 2 minutes until hot. Push to one side of the pan.

② Tilt the pan and pour the egg into the corner. Cook the egg, stirring and gradually drawing in the rice until it is flecked with tiny threads of egg.

③ Sprinkle with the five-spice powder and soy sauce. Stir and serve.

PREPARATION TIME: 2 MINUTES
COOKING TIME: 4–5 MINUTES

Desserts

Desserts don't necessarily spring to mind as being suitable for cooking in a frying pan (skillet). There are, of course, flambéed puddings and pancakes – and I've included a couple of these – but you can use a frying pan for a whole collection of tempting, sumptuous desserts that can be cooked more quickly and more easily than in a saucepan or in the oven.

Warm Tiramisu

SERVES 4

---

300 ml/½ pt/1¼ cups water
20 ml/1½ tbsp instant coffee granules
60 ml/4 tbsp brandy
4 trifle sponges
200 g/7 oz/scant 1 cup Mascarpone cheese
30 ml/2 tbsp icing (confectioners') sugar
120 ml/4 fl oz/½ cup double (heavy) or whipping cream, whipped
10 ml/2 tsp drinking (sweetened) chocolate powder

---

① Put the water, coffee and half the brandy in a frying pan (skillet). Heat, stirring, over a low heat until the coffee dissolves and the water is beginning to bubble.

② Add the trifle sponges. Soak on one side for about 30 seconds, then turn over and soak until nearly all the liquid has been absorbed,

③ Carefully transfer the sponges to glass dishes, using a large spoon (there may be little bits of soggy sponge left behind, but don't worry).

④ Add the Mascarpone cheese, icing sugar and remaining brandy to the pan and stir over a gentle heat until a pale coffee colour and just beginning to bubble.

⑤ Spoon over the sponges in the dishes. Top each with a dollop of whipped cream, sprinkle with the chocolate powder and serve straight away.

PREPARATION TIME: 3 MINUTES
COOKING TIME: 4–5 MINUTES

Bread and Butter Pan Pudding

SERVES 4

3 slices of white bread
Butter or margarine, for spreading
50 g/2 oz/⅓ cup mixed dried fruit (fruit cake mix)
40 g/1½ oz/3 tbsp caster (superfine) sugar
1.5 ml/¼ tsp freshly grated nutmeg
2 eggs
300 ml/½ pt/1¼ cups milk

① Spread the bread with butter or margarine and cut each slice into quarters. Place four quarters, buttered side down, in a medium frying pan (skillet) over a low heat.

② Sprinkle with a third of the fruit and sugar. Add four more quarters, buttered side up, then all the remaining fruit and half the remaining sugar.

③ Arrange the last quarters on top and sprinkle with the remaining sugar and the nutmeg.

④ Beat the eggs and milk together and pour over. Cover with a lid and cook gently for 20 minutes until set.

⑤ Flash under a preheated grill (broiler) to brown the top and serve warm, straight from the pan.

PREPARATION TIME: 8 MINUTES
COOKING TIME: 25 MINUTES

Flambéed Summer Fruits

SERVES 4

50 g/2 oz/¼ cup caster (superfine) sugar
30 ml/2 tbsp lemon juice
60 ml/4 tbsp water
350 g/12 oz mixed soft fruits, e.g. strawberries,
  raspberries, blackcurrants, etc.
45 ml/3 tbsp kirsch
To serve:
Crème fraîche

① Put the sugar, lemon juice and water in a frying pan (skillet). Heat, stirring, until the sugar dissolves, then boil for 1 minute.

② Add the fruits and cook gently for 3–4 minutes, stirring once or twice, until soft but still holding their shape.

③ Pour over the kirsch, ignite and shake the pan until the flames subside.

④ Serve hot with crème fraîche.

PREPARATION TIME: 2 MINUTES
COOKING TIME: 6–7 MINUTES

Crêpes Suzette

SERVES 4

I had to include this classic dish. You can use the pancake recipe on page 152 to make the crêpes if you prefer.

75 g/3 oz/¾ cup self-raising (self-rising) flour
1.5 ml/¼ tsp salt
15 ml/1 tbsp icing (confectioners') sugar
40 g/1½ oz/3 tbsp butter
1 egg, beaten
250 ml/8 fl oz/1 cup milk
Sunflower oil, for cooking
2 oranges
½ lemon
25 g/1 oz/2 tbsp light brown sugar
45 ml/3 tbsp Grand Marnier or brandy

① Sift the flour, salt and icing sugar together in a bowl.

② Melt 15 g/½ oz/1 tbsp of the butter. Make a well in the middle of the flour and add the melted butter and the egg. Gradually beat in the milk until smooth. Leave to stand for at least 1 hour.

③ Heat a little oil in a small frying pan (skillet). Pour off the excess. Add two tablespoonfuls of batter and swirl round the pan to coat the base thinly. Cook until golden underneath, then flip over and cook the other side. Slide out of the pan on to a plate over a pan of gently simmering water. Repeat until all the batter is used, reheating and oiling the pan between each pancake.

④ Thinly pare the rind of one orange, cut into strips and boil in water for 3 minutes, then drain. Rinse with cold water, drain again and reserve. Squeeze the juice from both oranges and the half lemon.

⑤ Melt the remaining butter in the frying pan. Add the sugar and orange and lemon juices. Heat, stirring, until the sugar melts, then allow to bubble for about 3 minutes until slightly thickening.

⑥ Fold each pancake into quarters. Add them to the pan, one at a time, spoon the sauce over and push to one side.

⑦ When all the pancakes are in the sauce, sprinkle the orange rind over and heat gently for 2 minutes. Pour the Grand Marnier or brandy over, ignite and serve straight away.

PREPARATION TIME: 15 MINUTES
COOKING TIME: 30 MINUTES

Pancakes with Pears and Chocolate Hazelnut Sauce
SERVES 4

1 quantity of pancake mixture (see page 152)
410 g/14½ oz/1 large can of pear quarters, drained and chopped
60 ml/4 tbsp chocolate and hazelnut (filbert) spread
60 ml/4 tbsp milk
30 ml/2 tbsp chopped toasted hazelnuts
To serve:
Vanilla ice cream or whipped cream

① Make up eight pancakes. Divide the pears among them and roll up. Place two pancakes on each of four plates.

② Put the chocolate spread and milk in the frying pan (skillet) and heat until blended and bubbling. Stir in the nuts. Spoon over the pancakes and serve with ice cream or whipped cream.

PREPARATION TIME: 15 MINUTES
COOKING TIME: 15–20 MINUTES
(INCLUDING COOKING PANCAKES)

Floating Islands
SERVES 4

50 g/2 oz/¼ cup butter
2 eggs, separated
100 g/4 oz/½ cup caster (superfine) sugar
15 ml/1 tbsp cornflour (cornstarch)
150 ml/¼ pt/⅔ cup double (heavy) cream
250 g/9 oz/1 medium can of crushed pineapple

① Melt the butter in a large frying pan (skillet). Whisk the egg yolks with 30 ml/2 tbsp of the sugar, the cornflour and the cream. Whisk in the melted butter and the can of crushed pineapple with its liquid. Return to the frying pan.

② Cook over a very gentle heat, stirring until thick. Remove from the heat.

③ Whisk the egg whites until stiff. Whisk in half the remaining sugar and whisk again. Fold in the remainder with a metal spoon.

④ Return the pan to a low heat. Drop eight spoonfuls of meringue over the buttery sauce. Cover with a lid or a dome of foil. Cook gently for 15 minutes until the meringues are set.

⑤ Serve straight from the pan, either hot or cold.

PREPARATION TIME: 10 MINUTES
COOKING TIME: 20 MINUTES

Tropical Bananas

SERVES 4

This is very rich, but absolutely scrumptious! Use the rest of the coconut milk in a curry or whizzed up with a banana and a little milk and honey for a delicious tropical milkshake.

4 bananas
15 g/½ oz/1 tbsp butter
45 ml/3 tbsp dark brown sugar
300 ml/½ pt/⅔ cup canned coconut milk
Finely grated rind and juice of 1 lime
30 ml/2 tbsp dark rum
4 slices of lime
To serve:
Whipped cream or vanilla ice cream

① Peel the bananas, cut into halves widthways, then cut each piece in half lengthways.

② Melt the butter in the frying pan (skillet). Add the bananas and fry (sauté) for just 1 minute on each side. Remove from the pan.

③ Add the sugar and stir until melted.

④ Add the coconut milk and lime rind and juice. Bring to the boil, stirring, then boil for 3–4 minutes until thickened, stirring all the time.

⑤ Return the bananas to the pan.

⑥ Pour the rum into a ladle, warm, then ignite. Pour over the bananas while flaming and shake the pan until the flames subside.

⑦ Spoon into glass dishes. Make a cut from the centre to the edge of each slice of lime and sit one slice over the rim of each dish. Top the bananas with some whipped cream or ice cream and serve straight away before the cream or ice cream melts.

PREPARATION TIME: 5 MINUTES
COOKING TIME: 7–8 MINUTES

Apple Fritters with Golden Sauce
SERVES 4

Try these with pineapple or bananas too.

90 ml/6 tbsp golden (light corn) syrup
30 ml/2 tbsp lemon juice
100 g/4 oz/1 cup plain (all-purpose) flour
5 ml/1 tsp baking powder
A pinch of salt
150 ml/¼ pt/⅔ cup water
3 eating (dessert) apples
Groundnut (peanut) or corn oil, for deep-frying
A little caster (superfine) sugar, for dusting

① Put the syrup and lemon juice in a small saucepan, ready to warm through.

② Sift the flour, baking powder and salt in a bowl. Stir in the water to form a thick batter.

③ Peel, core and thickly slice the apples.

④ Pour about 2 cm/¾ in oil in a large frying pan (skillet) and heat until a cube of day-old bread browns in 30 seconds.

⑤ Dip the slices of apple in the batter and drop gently into the hot oil. Fry (sauté), turning once, for about 3–4 minutes until crisp and golden. Drain thoroughly on kitchen paper (paper towels).

⑥ Warm the syrup sauce.

⑦ Pile the fritters on warm plates and dust with caster sugar. Trickle the syrup sauce over and serve straight away.

PREPARATION TIME: 15 MINUTES
COOKING TIME: 3–4 MINUTES

Spiced Caramelised Clementines
SERVES 4

Use any small, soft, easy-peel citrus fruit for this dish.

8 clementines
75 g/3 oz/⅓ cup caster (superfine) sugar
300 ml/½ pt/1¼ cups boiling water
2.5 ml/½ tsp mixed (apple-pie) spice
Juice of ½ lemon
To serve:
Crème fraîche

① Peel the fruit but leave whole.

② Put the sugar in a heavy-based frying pan (skillet). Heat, stirring, until the sugar melts and is a rich golden brown. Take care not to let it burn.

③ Pour in the boiling water (it will splutter and bubble up). Stir until the caramel melts, then stir in the mixed spice.

④ Stand the fruit in the pan, turn down the heat until just bubbling round the edges and cook for 10 minutes.

⑤ Carefully turn the fruit over and continue to cook for a further 10 minutes. Sprinkle the lemon juice over.

⑥ Serve either hot or cold with crème fraîche.

PREPARATION TIME: 8 MINUTES
COOKING TIME: 25 MINUTES

Arabian Cakes

SERVES 4

---

50 g/2 oz/½ cup sesame seeds
50 g/2 oz/¼ cup unsalted (sweet) butter
225 g/8 oz/1⅓ cups chopped cooking dates
Finely grated rind and juice of 1 lime
100 g/4 oz/1 cup plain (all-purpose) flour
50 g/2 oz/½ cup wholemeal flour
Sunflower oil, for cooking
150 ml/¼ pt/⅔ cup double (heavy) cream
10 ml/2 tsp rosewater
10 ml/2 tsp icing (confectioners') sugar
A few rose petals (optional)

---

① Put the sesame seeds in a frying pan (skillet). Heat, tossing gently, until golden. Tip out of the pan into a bowl.

② Wipe out the pan with kitchen paper (paper towels). Add the butter and heat until melted. Pour into the bowl and add the dates and the lime rind and juice. Mix well.

③ Stir in both the flours to form a firm paste. Shape the mixture into small cakes about 4 cm/1½ in in diameter.

④ Heat enough oil to cover the base of the frying pan. Cook the cakes for about 2–3 minutes on each side until golden brown. Drain on kitchen paper.

⑤ Meanwhile, whip the cream with the rosewater and icing sugar until peaking.

⑥ Arrange the little cakes on serving plates with a small pile of whipped rosewater cream to one side. Scatter with rose petals, if liked.

PREPARATION TIME: 15 MINUTES
COOKING TIME: 4–6 MINUTES

Lemon Soufflé Omelette
SERVES 4

If you don't have a grill (broiler), you can carefully turn the omelette over in the pan to cook the second side, but the result will be a little flat!

60 ml/4 tbsp lemon curd
3 eggs, separated
30 ml/2 tbsp water
15 g/½ oz/1 tbsp butter
30 ml/2 tbsp icing (confectioners') sugar
To serve:
Vanilla ice cream

① Put the lemon curd in a bowl and beat in the egg yolks and water.

② Whisk the egg whites until stiff. Fold into the lemon mixture with a metal spoon.

③ Heat the butter in a medium frying pan (skillet) until foaming and swirl round to coat the base.

④ Spoon the mixture into the pan and cook over a moderate heat for 3 minutes until golden underneath.

⑤ Place the pan under a preheated grill for about 2 minutes until the mixture is puffy and golden on top.

⑥ Dust with sifted icing sugar, cut into wedges and serve straight away with vanilla ice cream.

PREPARATION TIME: 5 MINUTES
COOKING TIME: 5 MINUTES

Whisky Crème Brûlée

SERVES 6

For this recipe, you need a very large frying pan (skillet) that will accommodate six ramekin dishes (custard cups). If necessary, use two pans – you'll still use far less fuel than cooking them in the oven. The leftover egg whites can be used for an egg and breadcrumb coating or, of course, for meringues. A standard large carton of cream – labelled 568 ml/20 fl oz – will be fine for this recipe.

2 whole eggs
2 egg yolks
175 g/6 oz/¾ cup caster (superfine) sugar
600 ml/1 pt/2½ cups double (heavy) cream
5 ml/1 tsp vanilla essence (extract)
45 ml/3 tbsp whisky

① Whisk the whole eggs, egg yolks and 30 ml/2 tbsp of the sugar together in a large bowl. Whisk in the cream, vanilla and whisky.

② Pour into six ramekin dishes. Put in a large frying pan and pour in enough boiling water to come halfway up the sides of the dishes. Bring back to the boil, then turn down the heat to low. Cover with a lid or foil and cook for about 30 minutes or until the custards are set.

③ Lift the dishes out of the pan and leave to cool, then chill.

④ Put the remaining sugar in a heavy-based frying pan. Heat, stirring gently, until the sugar melts and caramelises.

⑤ Pour immediately over the chilled custards and chill again until ready to serve.

PREPARATION TIME: 10 MINUTES
COOKING TIME: 35 MINUTES

Pan Breads, Scones and Cakes

You normally associate breads, scones (biscuits) and cakes with baking in the oven, but many are ideal for cooking in a pan. These recipes are a great way of showing you just how versatile your frying pan (skillet) can be and are perfect to make when time is of the essence.

Caraway Flat Breads
MAKES 6

You can make this dough in a food processor, but don't add the seeds straight away. Run the machine for 1 minute after the dough is formed to knead it, then add the seeds and run the machine again briefly to mix them in without chopping them up. The breads are fantastic eaten straight from the pan but can be reheated in a low oven or briefly in the microwave.

2.5 ml/½ tsp caster (superfine) sugar
1.5 ml/¼ tsp salt
225 g/8 oz/2 cups strong plain (bread) flour
10 ml/2 tsp easy-blend dried yeast
15 ml/1 tbsp caraway seeds
150 ml/¼ pt/⅔ cup hand-hot water
Sunflower oil, for greasing

① Sift the sugar, salt and flour into a bowl and stir in the yeast and caraway seeds.

② Gradually mix in enough of the water to form a soft but not sticky dough.

③ Knead gently on a lightly floured surface for 5 minutes until smooth and elastic.

④ Place the dough in an oiled polythene bag and leave in a warm place for about 45 minutes until doubled in bulk.

⑤ Knock back (punch down) the dough and divide into six equal pieces. Shape each into an 'egg' shape and roll out to an oval about 15 cm/6 in long. Lay them on a damp tea towel (dish cloth) and cover with another damp cloth. Leave to rest for 15 minutes.

⑥ Brush a heavy-based frying pan (skillet) with oil. Heat over a moderate heat for 1–2 minutes. Add two breads and cook for about 2– 2½ minutes until puffing up and lightly browned in places underneath. Flip over and cook the other sides for a further 2 minutes until lightly browned. Wrap in a napkin to keep warm while cooking the remainder. Serve warm.

PREPARATION TIME: 15 MINUTES PLUS RISING
COOKING TIME: 15–20 MINUTES

Pan Garlic Bread
SERVES 4

25 g/1 oz/2 tbsp butter
30 ml/2 tbsp sunflower oil
1 garlic clove, crushed
15 ml/1 tbsp chopped fresh parsley
5 ml/1 tsp dried oregano
8 slices of French bread

① Heat the butter and oil in a frying pan (skillet) until the butter melts. Stir in the garlic and herbs over a fairly gentle heat.

② Quickly turn the bread in the mixture to coat both sides. Fry (sauté) for about 2 minutes on each side until just beginning to turn golden at the edges but still soft in the middle.

③ Remove from the pan and serve straight away.

PREPARATION TIME: 5 MINUTES
COOKING TIME: 4–5 MINUTES

No-fat Tortillas
MAKES 12

These are great served as breads with any spicy foods – especially Mexican, of course. Alternatively, wrap them round a filling of your choice, such as chilli and shredded lettuce, or baked beans and grated cheese.

100 g/4 oz/1 cup medium oatmeal
100 g/4 oz/1 cup self-raising (self-rising) flour
2.5 ml/½ tsp baking powder
A good pinch of salt
250 ml/8 fl oz/1 cup hand-hot water

① Mix the oatmeal, flour, baking powder and salt together in a bowl.

② Mix with enough of the water to form a soft but not sticky dough.

③ Knead gently on a lightly floured surface.

④ Divide the dough into 12 balls. Dust the work surface with a mixture of oatmeal and flour and roll out each piece to a thin round.

⑤ Heat a heavy-based non-stick frying pan (skillet) until very hot. Add a tortilla and cook for 1–2 minutes on each side until dry and flecked with brown.

⑥ Keep warm in a napkin on a plate over a pan of hot water while cooking the remainder. Serve warm.

PREPARATION TIME: 10 MINUTES
COOKING TIME: 2–4 MINUTES PER TORTILLA

Cinnamon French Toast

SERVES 4

2 eggs
30 ml/2 tbsp milk
4 slices of white bread, crusts removed
25 g/1 oz/2 tbsp butter
30 ml/2 tbsp sunflower oil
30 ml/2 tbsp caster (superfine) sugar
2.5 ml/½ tsp ground cinnamon

1. Beat the eggs and milk together in a large, shallow dish.

2. Soak the bread on both sides in the egg and milk until thoroughly coated.

3. Heat half the butter and oil in a large frying pan (skillet). Add two slices of bread and fry (sauté) on both sides until golden.

4. Mix the caster sugar and cinnamon together in a shallow dish. Dip the fried bread in the sugar mixture to coat both sides. Cut into fingers.

5. Fry and coat the remaining bread in the same way.

6. Serve the fingers while still warm.

PREPARATION TIME: 5 MINUTES
COOKING TIME: 4–6 MINUTES

Staffordshire Oat Pancakes
MAKES 8

100 g/4 oz/1 cup plain (all-purpose) flour
50 g/2 oz/½ cup medium oatmeal
10 ml/2 tsp easy-blend dried yeast
5 ml/1 tsp caster (superfine) sugar
2.5 ml/½ tsp salt
450 ml/¾ pt/2 cups hand-hot milk and water, mixed
Sunflower oil, for cooking
To serve:
Butter and jam (conserve) or cheese

① Mix the flour, oatmeal, yeast, sugar and salt together in a bowl.

② Gradually mix in the hand-hot milk and water to form a batter.

③ Cover the bowl with clingfilm (plastic wrap) and leave the batter in a warm place for about 1 hour to rise.

④ Heat a little oil in a small heavy-based frying pan (skillet). Pour off the excess. Add 45 ml/3 tbsp of the batter to the pan and swirl round to coat the base of the pan thinly. Cook until golden underneath. Flip over and cook the other side. Keep warm on a plate over a pan of gently simmering water while cooking the remainder.

⑤ Serve hot, spread with butter and jam, or spread with butter and wrap round a piece of cheese.

PREPARATION TIME: 10 MINUTES PLUS RISING
COOKING TIME: 2–3 MINUTES PER OATCAKE

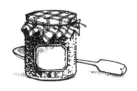

Crisp Oatcakes
MAKES 8

These are great served for breakfast with butter and marmalade or with cheese for a snack lunch or after dinner.

75 g/3 oz/¾ cup medium oatmeal, plus extra for dusting
1.5 ml/¼ tsp bicarbonate of soda (baking soda)
A good pinch of salt
15 g/½ oz/1 tbsp butter or margarine
60 ml/4 tbsp water
Sunflower oil, for greasing

① Mix the oatmeal with the bicarbonate of soda and salt in a bowl.

② Melt the butter or margarine in a large frying pan (skillet). Add the water and swirl round, then pour into the bowl of oatmeal mixture. Mix with a round-bladed knife to form a firm dough.

③ Knead together into a ball. Dust a work surface with extra oatmeal and roll out the dough to a large, thin round about 25 cm/10 in in diameter. Use a saucepan lid or dinner plate as a guide if necessary.

④ Cut into eight wedges.

⑤ Heat the frying pan to evaporate any residual water. Brush the surface with sunflower oil. Add four of the oatcakes and cook over a fairly gentle heat for about 3 minutes until firm. Carefully turn them over and cook the other side for a further 2 minutes. Transfer to a wire rack to cool. Re-grease and reheat the pan and cook the remainder.

⑥ When cold, store in an airtight container until ready to serve.

PREPARATION TIME: 15 MINUTES
COOKING TIME: 10 MINUTES

Chocolate Caramel Squares
MAKES 12

These are very sinful but a real treat for anyone with a sweet tooth. You can counter the sweetness by adding the grated rind of a lemon to the condensed milk mixture when cooking.

150 g/5 oz/⅔ cup butter, plus extra for greasing
100 g/4 oz/1 cup plain biscuits (cookies), crushed
400 g/14 oz/1 large can of sweetened condensed milk
30 ml/2 tbsp golden (light corn) syrup
100 g/4 oz plain (semi-sweet) chocolate

① Melt the butter in a large frying pan (skillet). Spoon 45 ml/ 3 tbsp into a bowl and add the biscuits. Mix together and press into a lightly greased 18 cm/7 in square, shallow baking tin (pan).

② Add the condensed milk and syrup to the butter remaining in the frying pan. Heat gently until boiling, stirring all the time, then continue to stir and boil for about 5 minutes until the mixture is golden and thick and the butter is completely blended in.

③ Spoon over the biscuits in the baking tin and spread out.

④ Wash the frying pan, then break up the chocolate and place in the pan. Heat gently, stirring until melted. Do not allow to boil. Spread over the caramel. Leave to cool, then chill overnight until firm. Cut into fingers and store in an airtight container.

PREPARATION TIME: 5 MINUTES
COOKING TIME: 9 MINUTES

Potato Scones
MAKES 10

450 g/1 lb potatoes, peeled and cut into pieces
7.5 ml/1½ tsp salt
50 g/2 oz/¼ cup butter or margarine, plus extra for
  spreading
100 g/4 oz/1 cup plain (all-purpose) flour
A little sunflower oil, for greasing

① Cook the potatoes in boiling water until tender. Drain well and mash thoroughly.

② Add the salt and butter or margarine and mix until melted. Work in the flour with a wooden spoon.

③ When cool enough to handle, turn out on a lightly floured surface and knead gently. Roll out to 1 cm/½ in thick and cut into small rounds, using a 5 cm/2 in cutter, re-shaping the trimmings to make the last few scones.

④ Lightly grease a heavy-based frying pan (skillet). Heat over a moderate heat. Cook the scones (biscuits) in two batches for 4–5 minutes on each side until golden and cooked through.

⑤ Serve warm, spread with butter or margarine.

PREPARATION TIME: 15 MINUTES
COOKING TIME: ABOUT 20 MINUTES (8–10 MINUTES PER BATCH)

Pan Eccles Cakes

MAKES 10

100 g/4 oz/1 cup plain (all-purpose) flour
A good pinch of salt
25 g/1 oz/2 tbsp white vegetable fat (shortening)
50 g/2 oz/¼ cup hard block margarine
A little cold water
1.5 ml/¼ tsp mixed (apple-pie) spice
Grated rind of ½ lemon
50 g/2 oz/⅓ cup raisins
10 ml/2 tsp caster (superfine) sugar, plus extra for
  dusting
30 ml/2 tbsp sunflower oil

① Mix the flour and salt in a bowl. Add the white fat and 25 g/1 oz/2 tbsp of the margarine, cut into pieces, and rub in with your fingertips until the mixture resembles breadcrumbs.

② Mix with enough cold water to form a soft but not sticky dough.

③ Knead gently on a lightly floured surface. Roll out fairly thinly and cut into 10 rounds using a 7.5 cm/3 in cutter, re-rolling and cutting the trimmings as necessary. Brush with water.

④ Melt the remaining margarine and stir in the mixed spice, lemon rind, raisins and measured caster sugar.

⑤ Spoon this mixture into the centres of the rounds of pastry (paste). Draw the pastry up over the filling and press the edges well together to seal. Turn over and roll the rounds gently with a rolling pin to flatten, so that you can see the raisins through the pastry.

⑥ Heat the oil in a large frying pan (skillet). Add the round cakes and cook for about 2 minutes until golden brown underneath. Turn over and cook for a further 2 minutes or until golden and cooked through. Transfer to kitchen paper (paper towels) to drain.

⑦ Dust with a little extra caster sugar and serve warm or cold.

PREPARATION TIME: 20 MINUTES
COOKING TIME: 4 MINUTES

Wheaten Drop Scones
MAKES ABOUT 12

100 g/4 oz/1 cup wholemeal flour
10 ml/2 tsp baking powder
15 ml/1 tbsp caster (superfine) sugar
1 egg
150 ml/¼ pt/⅔ cup milk
Sunflower oil, for cooking
Butter or margarine, for spreading

① Mix the flour, baking powder and sugar together in a bowl.

② Make a well in the centre. Add the egg and half the milk and beat until smooth. Stir in the remaining milk.

③ Heat a little oil in a large frying pan (skillet), then pour off the excess. Drop six spoonfuls of the batter into the pan and cook until golden underneath and bubbles rise and burst on the surface. Flip over and cook the other sides.

④ Keep warm in a napkin while cooking the remainder. Serve warm, spread with butter or margarine.

PREPARATION TIME: 10 MINUTES
COOKING TIME: 6–8 MINUTES (3–4 MINUTES PER BATCH)

Cheese Scones

MAKES 9

225 g/8 oz/2 cups self-raising (self-rising) flour
10 ml/2 tsp baking powder
A pinch of salt
A pinch of cayenne
75 g/3 oz/⅓ cup butter or margarine, cut into pieces
50 g/2 oz/½ cup Cheddar cheese, grated
5 ml/1 tsp lemon juice
75 ml/5 tbsp milk
Sunflower oil, for greasing
Butter, for spreading

① Mix the flour, baking powder, salt and cayenne in a bowl.

② Add the butter or margarine and rub in with your fingertips until the mixture resembles breadcrumbs. Add the cheese.

③ Mix the lemon juice and milk together and stir into the mixture to form a soft but not sticky dough.

④ Knead gently on a lightly floured surface. Pat out to about 1 cm/½ in thick. Cut into rounds, using a 5 cm/2 in cutter. Re-knead and cut the trimmings to make the last few scones (biscuits).

⑤ Brush a large frying pan (skillet) with oil and heat gently. When hot, add the scones and cook for about 10 minutes until golden underneath. Do not be tempted to turn up the heat or they will burn. Turn the scones over and cook the other side for a further 5 minutes until brown and cooked through. They will sound hollow if tapped gently on the base.

⑥ Serve warm, split and spread with butter.

PREPARATION TIME: 20 MINUTES
COOKING TIME: 15 MINUTES

Indian-style Pooris

MAKES 8

These make a nice change for breakfast – and you can make the dough the night before, ready to cook in the morning.

100 g/4 oz/1 cup wholemeal flour
100 g/4 oz/1 cup plain (all-purpose) flour
A good pinch of salt
50 g/2 oz/¼ cup white vegetable fat
100 ml/3½ fl oz/scant ½ cup water
Sunflower oil, for shallow-frying
Butter and honey, for spreading

① Mix the flours and salt together in a bowl and rub in the fat until the mixture resembles breadcrumbs.

② Mix with the water to form a soft but not sticky dough. Knead gently until smooth, then wrap in clingfilm (plastic wrap).

③ When ready to cook, divide the dough into eight balls and roll into flat, 10 cm/4 in rounds.

④ Heat enough oil to cover the base of a large frying pan (skillet). Add two pooris and cook for 1–2 minutes until very lightly browned underneath and drying out. Flip over and cook for a further 1 minute to brown the other side. Drain on kitchen paper (paper towels) and keep warm while cooking the remainder.

⑤ As soon as all the pooris are cooked, spread lightly with butter and honey and serve straight away.

PREPARATION TIME: 10 MINUTES
COOKING TIME: ABOUT 10 MINUTES (2–3 MINUTES PER BATCH)

English Raisin Muffins

MAKES 6

You can make up the dough balls and keep them in the fridge overnight, ready to be cooked and eaten fresh in the morning. Alternatively, once cooked, the muffins can be kept in an airtight container, then toasted whole, split and spread with butter. For plain muffins, simply omit the mace and raisins.

100 g/4 oz/1 cup plain (all-purpose) flour
100 g/4 oz/1 cup strong white (bread) flour
2.5 ml/½ tsp salt
10 ml/2 tsp easy-blend dried yeast
1.5 ml/¼ tsp ground mace
15 g/½ oz/1 tbsp butter or margarine
120 ml/4 fl oz/½ cup milk
120 ml/4 fl oz/½ cup water
50 g/2 oz/⅓ cup raisins
Cornflour (cornstarch), for dusting
Butter and honey, for spreading

① Mix the flours, salt, yeast and mace in a bowl.

② Melt the butter or margarine in a small saucepan. Add the milk and water and heat until warm to the touch but not unbearably hot.

③ Stir into the flour mixture and mix with a wooden spoon until the mixture forms a wet dough, using your hands when it becomes difficult with the spoon. Work in the raisins.

④ Cover the bowl with oiled clingfilm (plastic wrap) and leave in a warm place for about 45 minutes until the dough has doubled in bulk.

⑤ Knock back (punch down) the dough, then divide into six equal pieces. Dust your hands with cornflour and shape each piece into a ball. Place on an oiled baking (cookie) sheet, also dusted with cornflour. Cover with oiled clingfilm and leave to rise again for about 30 minutes.

⑥ Heat a heavy-based frying pan (skillet) until it feels hot when you hold your hand 5 cm/2 in above the base of the pan. Add three of the muffins and cook over a moderate heat for about 8 minutes on each side until the top and bottom are pale golden with a thick white band round the middle. Wrap in a napkin while cooking the remainder.

⑦ While still warm, pull apart and spread with butter and honey. Serve immediately.

PREPARATION TIME: 10 MINUTES PLUS RISING
COOKING TIME: ABOUT 30 MINUTES (16 MINUTES PER BATCH)

Scrumpets
MAKES 6

6 crumpets
50 g/2 oz/¼ cup butter or margarine
60 ml/4 tbsp icing (confectioners') sugar
100 g/4 oz sliced fresh strawberries (optional)

① Spread the crumpets on both sides with the butter or margarine, then dust liberally with the icing sugar.

② Heat a large frying pan (skillet). Add the crumpets and fry (sauté) for about 2 minutes on each side until golden and sizzling.

③ Serve hot on their own or topped with sliced fresh strawberries.

PREPARATION TIME: 5 MINUTES
COOKING TIME: 4 MINUTES

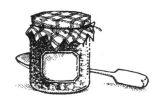

Pancakes
MAKES ABOUT 8

Serve these with lemon and sugar or syrup as a dessert or fill with any sweet or savoury mixture of your choice.

100 g/4 oz/1 cup plain (all-purpose) flour
A pinch of salt
1 egg
300 ml/½ pt/1¼ cups milk
Sunflower oil, for cooking

① Mix the flour and salt in a bowl.

② Make a well in the centre and add the egg and half the milk. Beat well to form a smooth batter. Stir in the remaining milk. Leave to stand for 30 minutes, if time allows.

③ Heat a little oil in a small frying pan (skillet). Pour off the excess.

④ Add 30–45 ml/2–3 tbsp batter and swirl round the pan to coat the base. Cook until just set and golden around the edges. Flip over and cook the other side.

⑤ Slide out of the pan and keep warm while cooking the remainder. Serve hot.

PREPARATION TIME: 8 MINUTES PLUS STANDING
COOKING TIME: 1–2 MINUTES PER PANCAKE

Pan-oh-chocolate

MAKES 6

These crisp, flaky crescents are a quick version of pain au chocolat, *which the French serve at breakfast. Cook them the night before, then refresh in a hot oven for a minute or two before serving. Personally, I find them too rich first thing in the morning – I prefer to serve them as a treat for tea or as a dessert, with crème fraîche.*

225 g/8 oz puff pastry (paste), thawed if frozen
45 ml/3 tbsp chocolate spread
Groundnut (peanut) or corn oil, for deep-frying
A little icing (confectioners') sugar, for dusting

① Cut the pastry into six equal pieces. Roll out each piece to a thin 15 cm/6 in square.

② Put 10 ml/2 tsp of chocolate spread in the centre of each square of pastry.

③ Brush the edges with water and fold over to form a triangle. Roll each one up, starting from the long edge, then curl round the points to form crescents.

④ Heat the oil until a cube of day-old bread browns in 30 seconds. Add the crescents and cook for 3–4 minutes until golden, puffy and cooked through. If they start to brown very quickly, turn down the heat slightly or the outsides will crisp before the centres are cooked.

⑤ Drain on kitchen paper (paper towels), then dust with icing sugar. Serve while still warm.

PREPARATION TIME: 10 MINUTES
COOKING TIME: 3–4 MINUTES

Index